PRODUCTIVITY ANALYSIS

STUDIES IN PRODUCTIVITY ANALYSIS,
Volume I

PRODUCTIVITY ANALYSIS
A Range of Perspectives

EDITED BY
Ali Dogramaci
Rutgers,
The State University
of New Jersey

Martinus Nijhoff Publishing
Boston/The Hague/London

Distributors for North America:
Martinus Nijhoff Publishing
Kluwer Boston, Inc.
190 Old Derby Street
Hingham, Massachusetts 02043

Distributors outside North America:
Kluwer Academic Publishers Group
Distribution Centre
P.O. Box 322
3300 AH Dordrecht, The Netherlands

Library of Congress Cataloging in Publication Data

Main entry under title:

Productivity analysis, a range of perspectives.

(Studies in productivity analysis; v. 1)
Includes bibliographies and indexes.
    1. Industrial productivity—United States—Addresses,
essays, lectures. I. Dogramaci, A. II. Series.
HD56.P818   338'.06'0973   80-14846

ISBN 0-89838-039-1

Printed in the United States of America

CONTENTS

8 PRODUCTIVITY AND ORGANIZATION MANAGEMENT   149

Leo B. Moore, *Massachusetts Institute of Technology,*
and Christine B. Moore

PREFACE

There is a wide variety of perspectives for productivity analysis. The backgrounds of different researchers and practitioners who work on this topic include such fields as economics, business administration, and industrial engineering, among others. Within each such field, there are different schools of thought on the theory and application of productivity analysis. Often it is not difficult to observe a lack of communication among the advocates of these separate schools. The purpose of this book is to present in a single volume samples of alternative approaches to productivity analysis. This may be considered as a first step toward a better communication among practitioners and researchers in the fields of management, industrial engineering, and economics. The focus of the book is on the United States, where the productivity growth problem has been acute for some time.

The book begins with a brief overview chapter that covers some of the issues involved in productivity analysis and a sample of methodological approaches presently in use. After this introduction, we move to Chapter 2 where Solomon Fabricant presents the issues related to measurement and analysis at the macroeconomic level.

In Chapter 3, C. Lowell Harriss discusses concepts that he considers essential for productivity growth: capital formation, technological progress, and freedom.

The fourth chapter is a study of the role of capital formation in U.S. productivity growth. The chapter is useful not only in terms of pointing out the importance of capital formation but also as a means of illustrating the application of total factor productivity concepts within the context of translog production functions. The approach of translog production functions, developed by Dale W. Jorgenson and his colleagues during the last decade, is used extensively by economists for industry studies and economic analyses at the national and international levels.

The next chapter is by Seymour Melman, who discusses three different modes of operation for organizations: cost minimization, cost pass-along, and cost maximization. The foundations of Melman's approach are different from those presented by Harriss in Chapter 3. This difference can serve as an indicator of the range of perspectives covered in the book. The wide-ranged spectrum demonstrates itself in a similar fashion throughout the rest of the volume.

In Chapter 6, we move to the Bela Gold school of thought, which has enjoyed many applications during the last twenty-five years. This chapter begins with a discussion of productivity measurement issues at the level of the firm. The sources of productivity adjustments and the effects of changes in technology and productivity relationships are discussed within the context of the Gold approach, and decision options are presented for implementation policies.

In Chapter 7, Martin K. Starr provides a management science approach. He analyzes several productivity problems within the framework of production management methodologies. He discusses operational issues of production processes and delineates some of the plant-level strategies for improving productivity performance.

The last chapter of the book is by Leo and Christine Moore. This chapter focuses on the human side of the enterprise and reflects some of the concerns of behavioral scientists regarding productivity issues.

Building bridges of communication between different schools of thought is not an easy task. This book is only a first attempt toward that objective. To the extent that similar attempts are made by others in the coming years, there may be hope for a better understanding in the future.

This book has greatly benefited from the suggestions of Philip D. Jones, director of Martinus Nijhoff Publishing, Boston, for which I am grateful. I am also grateful for the excellent supervision provided by Sarah Evans for the production of the manuscript and for the competent work of Jill O'Hagan who carried out the copy-editing work. I would like to thank Ballinger Publishing Company for their gracious permission to let us use in our Chapter 4 material from their book *Capital, Efficiency and Growth,* edited by George M. von Furstenberg, Copyright 1980, Ballinger Publishing Company. Similarly, I am thankful to Lexington Books. Figure 6.3 is printed with their permission.

I am indebted to my wife for her tolerance and support through the lengthy process of bringing this volume to completion and to my parents who helped and guided me throughout my educational process.

ACKNOWLEDGMENTS

The editor and contributing authors are deeply indebted to the referees for their invaluable comments and recommendations and for their numerous suggestions. We would like to express our deep personal appreciation for the thorough and constructive reviewing process provided by the referees whose names follow:

Ben Bernanke, Stanford University
John B. Donaldson, Columbia University
Nelson M. Fraiman, International Paper Company
John O. McClain, Cornell University
Campbell R. McConnell, University of Nebraska
I. Douglas Moon, Columbia University
Katherine Morgan, Montclair State College
Ishaq M. Nadiri, New York University
Peter V. Norden, IBM and Columbia University
Johannes M. Pennings, Columbia University
James L. Riggs, University of Oregon
George Sadler, American Productivity Center
James M. Suarez, Hunter College
Ephraim F. Sudit, Rutgers University

1 PERSPECTIVES ON PRODUCTIVITY

Ali Dogramaci

1.1. INTRODUCTION

In its last issue of 1979, the *Wall Street Journal* reported the following statement of William Batten, chairman of the New York Stock Exchange: "In 1960, the typical American worker in manufacturing annually produced as much as four Japanese workers or two French or German workers. Today, the American's output is matched by 1½ Japanese and by 1¼ Germans or Frenchmen. If the trend continues, all three will be outproducing us by the end of the next decade."

The decline in U.S. productivity growth is a phenomenon that is widely accepted. In their 1979 annual report, the Council of Economic Advisers to the president of the United States summed up the situation as follows: "Between 1948 and 1965, [labor] productivity growth in the private nonfarm sector averaged 2.6 percent per year. In 1966–73 this rate declined to 2.0 percent. Since 1973, private nonfarm productivity growth has averaged less than 1 percent per year."

There are different ways of measuring productivity, and one gets different numerical results depending on the specific meaning intended by the word *productivity* and on the method of calculation. Nevertheless, overall

U.S. productivity growth has declined so appreciably that within a wide spectrum of choices for the specific meaning of the word and for the method of calculation, an inescapable conclusion exhibits itself: The overall productivity growth of U.S. industries is in decline.

1.2. IMPORTANCE OF PRODUCTIVITY GROWTH

"Productivity refers to a comparison between the quantity of goods and services produced and the quantity of resources employed in turning out these goods or services" (Fabricant, 1969, p. 3). When productivity is defined in this general framework, the importance of productivity growth is explained by many researchers in many different dimensions.

Kendrick (1977, p. 5) begins his explanation of the significance of productivity growth by stating that a rise in productivity results in conservation in the use of scarce resources per unit of output. That is to say, to produce the same amount of output, we need to use a smaller amount of scarce resources. Productivity growth has also been related to a higher standard of living, since more output is produced per capita (Kendrick, 1977, p. 7; Kuznets, 1966; McConnell, 1979; National Center for Productivity and Quality of Working Life, 1978, pp. 5-6).

For the special case of labor productivity, Tatom (1979) explains the above reasoning by first defending the significance of output per worker for the firm. In his words, labor cost constitutes an important share of the total cost of production, and increased labor productivity may lead to lower unit costs of output. This in turn provides incentives for firms to increase production and leads to either one or both of the following two results: lower output prices and higher wages for employees. Pointing to the other side of the coin, McConnell (1979) states that because of the slowdown in its labor productivity, the United States no longer enjoys the highest per capita gross national product in the world.

Productivity growth has also been mentioned as having a bearing on inflation control. The National Center for Productivity and Quality of Working Life (1978, pp. 7-9) illustrated its case for labor productivity by comparing average annual percent changes during 1960-1967 with 1967-1977, as shown in Table 1.1. During the 1960-1967 period, unit labor cost increased slowly as compared to the period of 1967-1977 (1.1 percent versus 6.1 percent). The report related this to the small gap between the increase in rates of labor productivity and compensation during 1960-1967

Table 1.1.   Average Annual Percent Changes in Productivity and Inflation-Related Items for U.S. Private Business Sector

	Average Annual Percent Changes	
	1960–1967	*1967–1977*
Output/hour	3.7	1.6
Compensation/hour	4.9	7.8
Unit labor cost	1.1	6.1
Real hourly compensation	3.2	1.5
Consumer price index	1.7	6.3

SOURCE: National Center for Productivity and Quality of Working Life, 1978.

(3.7 percent versus 4.9 percent) and to the large gap between the same items during 1967–1977 (1.6 percent versus 7.8 percent). It was also pointed out that the rate of increase in consumer prices (1.7 percent versus 6.3 percent in the two respective periods) was affected by the above changes. The linkage between productivity slowdown and inflation has also been mentioned by Brennan (1978), Council of Economic Advisers (1980), Glaser (1976), Grayson (1978), Harriss (1975, p. 14), Malkiel (1979), McConnell (1979), New York Stock Exchange (1979), and Riggs (1972, p. 623).

International competitiveness is another factor that has been considered by many researchers to be under the influence of productivity performances. Melman (1956) pointed out that the higher level of labor productivity in the United States as compared to other industrialized nations enabled American workers to receive substantially higher wages than workers in other countries. Furthermore, because of high labor productivity, U.S. industries were able to maintain their competitive position in international markets in spite of their high wage rates. However, through time the situation changed, and by 1965 Melman was already calling attention to it (Melman, 1965). A brief picture of the more recent growth rates of labor productivity in manufacturing industries (which are a subset of the private business sector mentioned in Table 1.1) is given in Table 1.2 for eight industrialized countries; it shows the rates of change of other countries in a comparative way.

In terms of absolute magnitude of labor productivity, the United States still has an edge over most of the other countries. Output per worker is still high. However, what Table 1.2 shows is that unless the growth rates change substantially, other countries are likely to surpass the United States.

Table 1.2. Output per Man-Hour Indexes in Eight Countries (1967 = 100)

Countries	Years					
	1967	1970	1975	1976	1977	1978
United States	100	104.5	118.2	123.4	127.2	128.0
France	100	121.2	150.7	163.6	171.7	180.2
F.R. Germany	100	116.1	151.3	160.3	169.0	175.1
Italy	100	121.7	152.9	165.9	167.8	172.7
Netherlands	100	134.0	181.1	199.1	206.7	217.3
United Kingdom	100	110.0	126.1	129.2	128.2	130.5
Japan	100	146.5	174.6	188.7	197.3	212.9
Canada	100	114.7	133.7	140.4	148.1	155.0

SOURCE: U.S. Department of Commerce, 1979.

As U.S. productivity growth slips relative to some of the other industrialized countries, its international competitiveness tends to be affected unfavorably (Melman, 1974, pp. 84–95; National Center for Productivity and Quality of Working Life, 1978, pp. 9–11). The implications to international trade and the U.S. balance of payments have been mentioned by Kendrick (1977), McConnell (1979), New York Stock Exchange (1979), and Samuelson (1973, p. 716).

Productivity increases in an economy have also been viewed as a dynamic feedback process. In a recent article, Hulten (1979) pointed out the dynamic implications of productivity growth. He stated that the importance of productivity increases in a given period is not only the increase in output we obtain as inputs are used more efficiently but also the implications for the future: The increase in output during a given period leads to additional savings and capital formation. In turn, this additional growth of capital stock further improves the productivity picture in future years.

Proponents of productivity growth have also stated that as productivity improves, work may tend to absorb a smaller amount of time per year and per lifetime as well. Thus a greater portion of our time may be devoted to leisure (Kendrick, 1973, p. 3; Samuelson, 1973, p. 81), and a stronger support may be provided for an aging population (National Center for Productivity and Quality of Working Life, 1978, p. 12).

Finally, we may note that increase in productivity does not always mean sacrifices in environmental and ecological qualities. There are methods for improving productivity that do not cause pollution or higher accident rates.[1] Furthermore, some authors have stated that when we improve productivity, the extra income produced can be used to control or even to reverse environmental pollution without sacrificing other goals (Kendrick, 1977, p. 7 and 1973, p. 2; National Center for Productivity and Quality of Working Life, 1978, p. 12).

In brief, many authors have supported viewpoints that increases in productivity growth *may* lead to such benefits as higher standards of living, less inflation, improved balance of trade, further productivity growth, greater leisure time, better support for an aging population, and even environmental improvements. However, these relationships are not universally accepted. For example, Gold (1975, p. 1) has reservations about the relationships listed above. In his view, while one should be concerned with the productivity slowdown, one need not expect that the benefits listed above necessarily follow increases in output measures per input used. In his criticism, Gold points out that most of the other authors rely on aggregate economic studies and that many of the analyses are based on "production functions" (an approach not favored by Gold, 1975, pp. 170–72).

It should also be stressed that many of the researchers cited in this section who advocate improvement of U.S. productivity growth do not necessarily imply a "one-to-one" cause-effect relation between productivity growth and the outcomes listed above. For some, the results of productivity increases depend on what is specifically meant by the word *productivity* and how the increases are achieved. For some schools of thought, the costs of efforts for increasing productivity, the changes required in the industrial structure, the immediate or short-term implications for social and environmental conditions, or the time lags involved are factors that are sometimes weighted differently. Such factors lead to differences in the attractiveness of alternative solution strategies. The choice of a specific solution strategy may reflect the values or the preference structure of the decisionmaker; or it may reflect the decisionmaker's belief about the relationships between different variables and thus the effectiveness of different strategies for increasing productivity; or it may simply imply different interpretations of the concept of productivity.

1.3. THE MEASUREMENT OF PRODUCTIVITY

The way in which productivity is measured determines the meaning that it carries. There are many different methods by which productivity is measured. Our objective in this section is to provide a brief introduction to some of the approaches.

1.3.1. Output per Man-Hour

The productivity figures presented in the annual reports of the Council of Economic Advisers are based on the output per man-hour series prepared by the Bureau of Labor Statistics (BLS). We shall begin our brief survey of productivity measures with the topic of labor productivity.

The Bureau of Labor Statistics computes its series for output per man-hour for the private sector as the ratio of "Gross Domestic Product originating in the private or individual sectors" to "the corresponding hours of all persons employed." The output figures are deflated to constant dollar values by adjusting them with price indexes.

In a recent article, Rees (1979) described some of the problems associated with these price indexes. A car that previously included a radio as optional equipment only may in later years have it included as standard equipment. Bureau of Labor Statistics price indexes judge the car to be improved and consider the output to be increased by the cost of the radio. On the other hand, this system may not make adequate adjustments for improvements in products for which quality has improved and for which at the same time costs have decreased as a result of technological developments. Rees (1979) cited the replacement of electromechanical desk calculators costing about $1000 by electronic calculators that do the same job faster and more quietly and yet cost $200. The Bureau of Labor Statistics treats the electronic calculators as a new product, when linking them to the price index, to show no price change at the transition. Rees stated, "If the number of new calculators produced equaled the former production of old calculators, the present procedure would show a drop in real output of calculators of 80 percent." As the chairman of the Panel to Review Productivity Statistics (National Academy of Sciences), Rees added, "This panel recommended that the Bureau of Labor Statistics seek to develop auxiliary measures of price changes that take into account types of quality change that are not now measured." Before closing this topic we should add that Rees (1979) also stated that the imperfections in the presently used labor productivity measures are not large enough to account for the productivity slowdown of the United States. He concluded, "Even if the measurement techniques had been improved 10 years earlier, productivity growth would still have dropped during the decade" (Rees, 1979, p. 27).

In the next chapter, Fabricant discusses these and some of the other problems related to the U.S. private sector output per man-hour indexes constructed by the BLS, including the following: the effect of varying inflation rates on output measures; the impact of imperfections in productivity measurement on indexes for the service industry; and the fact that government services are not included in the BLS index mentioned above (see Fabricant, 1969, pp. 20-21 as well).

1.3.2. Total Factor Productivity

Another index mentioned in the later chapters of this book is the index for total factor productivity. This index has gone through various stages of growth and application through the efforts of many researchers, including Abramovitz (1956), Kendrick (1956, 1961), Solow (1957), Fabricant (1959), Denison (1962), Griliches and Jorgenson (1966), Jorgenson and Griliches (1967), Christensen and Jorgenson (1969), and others.

Basically, total factor productivity is the ratio of "quantity of output produced" to "a weighted combination of quantities of different input factors used." Denoting total factor productivity by A and the level of production activity by V, we have

$$A = \frac{V}{\sum_{i=1}^{n} W_i x_i}, \tag{1.1}$$

where x_i is the quantity of input factor i and W_i is some appropriate weight, for $i = 1, 2, \ldots, n$. For two types of inputs, capital (K) and labor (L), the expression becomes

$$A = \frac{V}{(W_L \cdot L + W_K \cdot K)}. \tag{1.2}$$

The "arithmetic index" for total-factor-productivity *growth rate* (v) from base period 0 to period 1 is expressed as (Kendrick, 1961):

$$v = \frac{dA}{A} = \frac{\dfrac{V_1}{V_0}}{\dfrac{(W_L \cdot L_1 + W_K \cdot K_1)}{(W_L \cdot L_0 + W_K \cdot K_0)}} - 1, \tag{1.3}$$

where dA indicates the rate of change of total factor productivity with respect to time, 0 is the base period, and 1 is the current period. Nadiri (1970) points out that such an arithmetic index of growth rate of total factor productivity is consistent with a production function of the form

$$V = \frac{b \cdot K \cdot L}{(cL^\rho + dK^\rho)^{1/\rho}}, \tag{1.4}$$

where b, c, d, and ρ are specific parameters.

A more widely used index for total-factor-productivity growth rate is one first introduced by Solow (1957) and called the "geometric index" of total-factor-productivity growth rate. It is defined as:

$$v = \frac{dV}{V} - (W_L \frac{dL}{L} + W_K \frac{dK}{K}), \tag{1.5}$$

where dV, dL, and dK denote the rate of change in the quantities of V, L, and K with respect to time.

From the definition of natural logarithms,

$$\frac{d\ell n x}{dx} = \frac{1}{x}, \text{ and thus } d\ell n x = \frac{dx}{x}. \tag{1.6}$$

Total-factor-productivity growth rate can be expressed as (Christensen and Jorgenson, 1970):

$$v = d\ell n\, V - [W_L \cdot d\ell n L + W_K \cdot d\ell n K], \tag{1.7}$$

which leads to the analytical framework used by Fraumeni and Jorgenson in Chapter 4.

Index of total factor productivity is also called by many economists "index of technical change." Since equation 1.7 is based on logarithms, it is also referred to as "translog index of technical change." The production function underlying this index is the translog production function, developed by Christensen, Jorgenson, and Lau (1971, 1973). It is more general and comprehensive than the production function underlying the arithmetic index of total-factor-productivity growth. Many other production functions, including the Cobb-Douglas function used by Solow (1957), are special cases of the translog function.

Within the context of the geometric index of total-factor-productivity growth, there are many different ways by which researchers have measured the input factors and thus obtained different results. One of the big controversies took place between Denison, on one side, and Jorgenson and Griliches, on the other.[2] When measuring output, Denison prefers to subtract from the value of goods and services produced the depreciation amount for capital stock. Jorgenson and Griliches, on the other hand, prefer a different approach. They measure output on the left-hand side of the equation in gross terms, without subtracting depreciation from it. But on the right-hand side, capital input is measured in a way so as to: (1) incorporate the effects of taxation of income from capital; (2) account for the differences in rates of return and depreciation for different classes of assets and legal forms of organizations; (3) account for differences in rates of return due to price changes of different assets; and (4) handle the depreciation and replacement of capital stock in a manner that is internally consistent.

Denison's approach does not treat these four issues. There are also other issues where these two schools of thought differ, but we shall not go into them here.

The role of capital in U.S. productivity performance has also been studied by Clark (1978, 1979), Fabricant (1977), Norsworthy and Harper (1981), and Malkiel (1979); in Chapter 4, Fraumeni and Jorgenson will present a condensed outline of a detailed study they recently carried out on this topic.

1.3.3. Bela Gold's Approach

As in sections 1.3.1 and 1.3.2, we will present a brief summary of certain aspects of yet another school of thought in productivity analysis, the approach of Bela Gold and his colleagues. For a more comprehensive coverage on this topic, we refer the reader to Gold (1955, 1964, 1971, 1977, 1979 and Eilon, Gold, and Soesan (1976).

Gold points out that the objective of a firm is not to maximize physical output relative to physical inputs. He states that to understand the phenomena underlying the behavior of productivity measures, one should view them as a part of a linkage system: a linkage system that ties physical productivity measures to such managerial criteria as return on investment or profitability.

As a means of analyzing the network, "managerial control ratios" are developed. One set of such ratios are as follows (Gold, 1979, p. 51):

$$\frac{\text{profit}}{\text{total investment}} = \left(\frac{\text{profit}}{\text{output}}\right) \times \left(\frac{\text{output}}{\text{total investment}}\right). \tag{1.8}$$

That is to say, the movement of the ratios profit/output and output/investment are proposed to serve as decomposed indicators when one analyzes the ratio profit/investment.

Together with equation 1.8, Gold uses five more managerial control ratios as a base for planning and evaluation efforts of management (Gold, 1976, p. 22–23). They are

$$\frac{\text{profit}}{\text{total investment}} = \left(\begin{array}{cc}\text{average} & \text{average} \\ \text{price} & - \text{unit cost}\end{array}\right) \times \left(\begin{array}{c}\text{capacity} \\ \text{utilization} \\ \text{rate}\end{array}\right)$$

$$\times \left(\begin{array}{c}\text{productivity} \\ \text{of fixed} \\ \text{investment}\end{array}\right) \times \left(\begin{array}{c}\text{internal} \\ \text{allocation} \\ \text{of capital}\end{array}\right), \tag{1.9}$$

where

Average price = value of products/output;
Average unit cost = total costs/output;
Capacity utilization rate = output/capacity;
Productivity of fixed investment = capacity/fixed investment;
Internal allocation of capital = fixed investment/total investment.

From this network, total cost per output is linked to three ratios: wages/output, fixed cost/output, and material cost/output.

Finally, the cost ratios are tied to a network of direct input factors (displayed in Figure 6.1), consisting of three interrelated nodes: output per man-hour, output per input material volume, and capacity per fixed investment. The relationship between the cost ratios mentioned above and this last network of direct input factors is provided through decomposition relations, such as wage cost per output = (man-hours/output) × (wage rate per man-hours). Similarly, input material cost per output serves as an intermediary linkage between the network of direct input factors and equation 1.9. The linkage is studied through the decomposition of input material cost per output into input material volume/output and input material prices.

Gold studies the interactions between productivity adjustments and factor prices through equations of the following type (Gold, 1973):

$$
\left(\Delta \frac{\text{total costs}}{\text{output}}\right)_{1-2} = \left[\left(\Delta \frac{\text{wage costs}}{\text{output}}\right)_{1-2} \left(\frac{\text{wage cost}}{\text{total cost}}\right)_1\right]
$$
$$
+ \left[\left(\Delta \frac{\text{material cost}}{\text{output}}\right)_{1-2} \left(\frac{\text{material cost}}{\text{total cost}}\right)_1\right]
$$
$$
+ \left[\left(\Delta \frac{\text{other costs}}{\text{output}}\right)_{1-2} \left(\frac{\text{other costs}}{\text{total cost}}\right)_1\right]. \tag{1.10}
$$

Numerical examples for application of such approaches are given in Eilon, Gold, and Soesan (1976).

1.3.4. Wassily Leontief's Input-Output Model

In the basic Leontief (1951) input-output model, the production and consumption of n sectors (or industries) of an economy are represented by

$$
\sum_{i=1}^{n} (1 - \delta_{ij}) x_{ij} - X_j = 0, \tag{1.11}
$$

for $j = 1,2, \ldots, n$, where

X_j = Net output of sector (or industry): total output of sector j minus the amount of that output consumed within sector j itself;

x_{ij} = Output of sector j consumed by sector i;

$\delta_{ij} = 0$ if $i \neq j$, and 1 if $i = j$.

Defining a_{ij} for $i, j = 1, \ldots, n$, as coefficients of production (or input coefficient of product of sector i into sector j), a linear production function is introduced as follows:

$$x_{ij} = \frac{a_{ij}}{A_i A_j} X_i, \qquad (1.12)$$

for $i, j = 1,2, \ldots, n$.

For a base period, all A_i and A_j can be set equal to 1.0. Improvements in productivity and therefore changes in the relation between X_i and x_{ij} would be reflected by assigning proper values to A_i and A'_j in the later periods.

Substituting equation 1.12 in 1.11 yields

$$\sum_{i=1}^{n} (1 - \delta_{ij}) \frac{a_{ij}}{A_i A_j} X_i - X_j = 0, \qquad (1.13)$$

for $j = 1,2, \ldots, n$.

A_i is called the productivity coefficient of industry i. A'_i is called productivity coefficient of commodity i. If A_i increases, it means that to produce each unit of X_i, we need less resources from other industries. On the other hand, if A_i remains the same but A'_i increases, it means that each unit of output from industry i has become more efficient, and so the other industries can do the same job with less amounts of X_i.

Leontief (1951) illustrates the concepts by giving an example from the coal industry. Suppose k denotes the coal industry. Increase in A_k implies that we have productivity improvements in the mining of coal—that is, with the same amount of manpower, materials, and so forth, we can produce more coal. Increase in A'_k means each ton of coal produced will provide more energy than before. "If A_k and A'_k were to change proportionally, but in opposite directions, $A_k \cdot A'_k$ would remain the same. If the productivity of the coal mining industry had fallen to one-half its original level, but the combustion technique at the time had improved so as to reduce proportionally the amount of coal required in the production of any other commodity, the efficiency of the commodity coal, considered from the viewpoint of the economic system as a whole would remain unchanged" (Leontief, 1951, p. 64).

The power of Leontief's model in analyzing the complex interdependencies between different sectors of an economy turned out to be so attractive that in spite of the restrictive assumptions on which it had to rely (such as equation 1.12), in a short period of time its applications spread to a large number of countries and had a variety of purposes. The study of technological change and its effect on productivity is just one of the many different purposes for which it has been used (Leontief, 1966, 1977). Another example of its use is in the United Nations (1973) report prepared by A. G. Armstrong, where value added is expressed in terms of the primary inputs of an economy, within the context of an input-output model. A Laspeyres base weighted index of this value is obtained for any current year t. The same is done for a quantity index of primary inputs in year t, and a productivity index is developed from the ratio of the two (United Nations, 1973, p. 145–150).

Recent overviews of input-output models, their limitations, and their usage in productivity analyses have been provided by Edrilek (1977) and Moon (1981).

1.3.5. Productivity Measurement and Production Management

In the field of production management, productivity analysis is not performed at the macroeconomic level. The focus is on the firm, the service organization, the factory, or a smaller unit.

Except for publications on time-and-motion studies, the literature of production management does not use the term *productivity* as frequently as it could. Even though many of the studies in this field are directed toward the improvements of some productivity measure, researchers have often preferred to use such terminology as *minimization of makespan, average outgoing quality limit,* and so forth. And when they have had to use more general objectives, they have used such terms as *minimization of costs* more often than *maximization of system productivity.* Most of these terms are productivity measures in one way or the other. They are narrower but quite specific in meaning and application.

To explain the term *minimization of makespan,* we need to go back to the scheduling problem referred to in Section 1.2, note 1, where n jobs are waiting to be processed by any one of m machines. The setup times for the jobs depend on how the jobs are sequenced, and the objective is to find the sequence for which the sum of the setup times is a minimum. *Makespan* refers to the completion time of the whole set of jobs. So, minimization of makespan would mean improvement of both capital and labor productivity (a wide variety of such measures and algorithms to achieve them are presented in standard production management texts [Baker, 1974; Riggs, 1972; Starr 1978]).

As a second example, consider *average outgoing quality limit* (AOQL), a term used in statistical quality control. It refers to the maximum value of the average percentage of defective items leaving a production facility. The lower the value of AOQL, the higher will be the percentage of nondefective items. In general, statistical quality control methods attempt to improve the productivity of a system by reducing the number of defective items produced. And yet a book on this topic may not use the word *productivity* at all (Grant and Leavenworth, 1972).

Indeed the word *productivity* does not appear in the table of contents or subject index of many books on production management, even though they deal with methods for improving productivity (Wild, 1972; Muther, 1973; Francis and White, 1974; Johnson, Nevell, and Vergin, 1974), and even an economist, such as Jorgenson, when writing a book on a related topic, has conformed to this tendency and has used micro terminology (Jorgenson, McCall, and Radner, 1967). In brief, measurement and improvement of productivity in the production management literature of industrial engineering, management science, and operations research are often performed in narrow and highly specialized contexts. In many instances, this has been accompanied by a tendency to avoid such terms as *labor* and *capital productivity*. Some exceptions to this trend are the works of Hines (1976), Riggs (1972, 1978), and Starr (1973, 1978).

The above discussion excluded the field of time-and-motion study. Within this framework, labor productivity has been the major point of interest and can be measured by comparing the actual amount of time required to produce an item with the standard time. The standard time includes the normal time plus an allowance factor for unavoidable delays, fatigue, and personal needs of the worker. The normal time is established through time-and-motion studies that run as follows: The worker performs the job in the way determined by previous motion studies. The time required to carry out the tasks is recorded by a person with a stopwatch (or with other equipment, such as videotape cameras). The time worked during the experiment is divided by the number of units produced. The ratio obtained is multiplied by a performance-rating factor (determining the performance-rating factor is perhaps more an art than a science). Although the resulting indexes are mostly used for individual products or components manufactured by a plant, their extensions have been applied toward establishing overall productivity trends for firms (Mundel, 1978, p. 17). Time-

and-motion studies have also been used in the service industries (including dental clinics, law firms, etc.). Other techniques in this field include the ratio-delay method and predetermined standards (Mundel, p. 17).

1.3.6. Productivity Measures in Behavioral Sciences

In contrast to the literature of production management, the literature of behavioral sciences uses the term *productivity* quite frequently. Behavioral scientists study human behavior in a variety of forms of organizations and social settings. For many researchers in this field, such performance measures as personnel turnover, absenteeism, accident rates, and grievances are considered productivity criteria as much as such measures as production rate or quality of items produced (Katzell, Bienstock, and Faerstein, 1977). Usage of the term *productivity* in the more conventional sense, such as labor productivity, physical output per worker, and holding quality constant (*Work in America,* 1973; Sutermeister, 1976), has grown parallel to the more flexible interpretation of the meaning.

In the operational sense, the practice of measuring productivity has also varied considerably. On one side of the spectrum are somewhat subjective measures of productivity. For example, in a well-known study of motivation and productivity, Georgopoulos, Mahoney, and Jones (1957) collected their data through questionnaires filled out by the workers. The measure used to ascertain the productivity levels was based on the question: "What productivity percentage figure do you usually hit in a day? (Write in the percent below) _____ percent."

On the other side of the spectrum, there are behavioral science studies that rely on less subjective measures. However, such productivity measures vary from one project to another. Two examples that illustrate this follow:

The first example is from the study of Kimberly and Nielsen (1975) of an assembly line in the automotive industry. Productivity was defined in terms of the number of units produced per month and by the number of parts that had to be reworked (rejects from quality control). Both variables were measured by their means and standard deviations over a forty-one-month period to examine the effects of some organization development activities. Profitability of the plant was also evaluated. It may be noted that these measures are not ratios of output to some labor or capital input but rather measures of output per se. Extent of variations (if any) in man-hours or capital equipment in the plant, during the forty-one-month period were not explicitly accounted for.

The second example is from King's (1974) study of four plants, each folding and packaging clothing patterns. Monthly production rates and number of crews and workers were observed for each plant for twelve months. The issue investigated in this study is interesting. Managers were given artificial reports about previous findings obtained in implementing job enlargement and job enrichment programs. Led to expect higher productivity as a result of these organizational innovations, the managers increased their plant output during the experiment period (as compared to other plants whose managers were not fed the artificial reports on high productivity). Managers' expectations were found to be more important sources of variation than the innovation itself.

More recently there has been an inclination in this field to use larger numbers of performance measures in order to record the effects of organizational changes in a multidimensional system (Freeman and Jucker, 1981).

1.4. MORE ON THE RANGE OF PRODUCTIVITY ANALYSIS

The brief list of different approaches to productivity measurement given in the previous section covers only a part of the available methods. There are, in addition, other important approaches and applications, such as the works of Farrell (1957), Johansen (1961, 1972), Dhrymes (1963), Kendrick and Creamer (1965), Salter (1966), Aigner and Chu (1968), Finger (1971), Afriat (1972), Craig and Harris (1973), Greenberg (1973), Pratten (1976a, 1976b), Jorgenson and Lau (1981), Fraiman (1978), Abernathy (1978), Schmidt and Lovell (1979), Nadiri and Schankerman (1979), and Sato (1981).

In terms of areas of application related to productivity analysis, there are also other topics we did not mention. One such field is research and development. The linkage between research and development and productivity change has been studied in different ways by Gold (1977), Mansfield (1968, 1971, 1977), Nadiri (1979), and Terleckyj (1974), among others. A recent survey of some of the methodological issues pertaining to the production function approach and issues related to this field was provided by Griliches (1979). Again recently, a different method of analysis and perspective on the dilemma between technological change, innovation, and productivity growth was put forward by Abernathy (1978).

One of the important avenues in which future research and development can contribute to productivity growth is the generation of technologies to modify the present level of complementarity of energy and capital. (This may be difficult but not impossible. Compare the first or second generation of computers with the present ones. The present ones are more productive, cheaper to produce, and more energy efficient.) To the extent that energy and capital are complementary, improvement of U.S. labor productivity growth becomes a difficult task in face of rising energy prices. The importance of the problem is reflected in the works of Berndt and Jorgenson (1978) and Hudson and Jorgenson (1978). While Denison (1979b) maintains that the negative effect of energy price increase on U.S. productivity growth rate from 1973 to 1976 has been quite small, Jorgenson (1979a) has strongly argued that the ever rising energy prices dampen economic growth. The complementarity of energy and capital is a question that may not be easily resolved (Berndt and Wood, 1979). Considering the urgency of the problem, it seems safe to say that the energy crisis provides to engineers and economists a strong potential for closer cooperation in this field of productivity analysis and planning.

Another field where different disciplines have focused on a common area of interest is that of industrial relations and collective bargaining. The difficulties of productivity measurement and the related issues in collective bargaining (Gitlow, 1964) are of interest to a large number of people. Textbooks on personnel administration and the law (Greenman and Schmertz, 1979) and industrial relations (Beal, Wickersham, and Kienast, 1972) imply that finding techniques or technologies to improve productivity may not be enough. Industrial relations and the collective bargaining processes may play significant roles in implementation and translation of those developments into actual productivity growth. It is not difficult to visualize cases where the legal system can be an important determinant in fostering or impeding productivity growth (Farnsworth, 1975). The personnel factor can play a role in different ways as well. Examples of alternative decision-making structures in organizations were illustrated by Melman (1958, 1971), who showed that comparatively high productivity performances can be achieved in industrial enterprises having quite different modes of decision making. In a different perspective, studies by Riggs (1979, 1980) on productivity challenges and confrontations versus harmony in industrial relations provide examples of productivity performance under different modes of worker-management relations.

1.5. CONCLUDING REMARKS

There is a wide range of perspectives for productivity analysis. The variation in basic frameworks for productivity measurement is only one of the many reasons that account for the differences in the approaches. Contributing to the differences in the approaches are the indexes used for deflating values (Laspeyres, Paasche, Divisia, Log-Index [Sato, 1976], etc.); the way other variables are measured (e.g., measurement of capital); the choice of variables to be included in the analysis for possible determinants of productivity; the degrees of aggregation; the choice of functional forms for relationships between the variables; the specific backgrounds of different researchers; and the subareas and issues addressed.

In the following seven chapters, leading scholars in a variety of fields will present some of their thoughts on productivity issues. Even though the spectrum of different approaches to productivity analysis will not be fully covered, we hope that the sample provided in this book will serve to highlight some of the important features in different schools of thought.

NOTES

1. As an example, consider the following production-scheduling problem: A production facility has m number of identical machines. The work to be carried out consists of n different jobs. We want to minimize the sum of the setup times of n jobs. Each job has to be processed by (any) one of m identical machines. The setup time for any job depends on which other job was on the same machine just before. The sequence in which we process the jobs is the only factor that can vary the setup times. After a machine is set up for a job, processing takes place. The processing times are not affected by the way we sequence the jobs. By finding a schedule that minimizes the total setup time, we increase both the productivity of the machines and their workers and also deliver the completed jobs to the customers sooner. To find the optimal schedule, very large numbers of different sequences need to be investigated. For most problems, complete enumeration is not feasible; it would take many years for the fastest computer to enumerate all the different schedules for twenty jobs on a single machine. There exist some powerful scheduling algorithms that can solve a limited class of problems. Research for developing better scheduling algorithms could improve productivity without causing pollution or other environmental problems.

2. The collection of papers on this debate appeared in *Survey of Current Business,* vol. 52, no. 5, May 1972, Part 2 (Jorgenson and Griliches, 1967, 1972a, 1972b; Denison, 1969, 1972).

REFERENCES

Abernathy, William J., 1978, *The Productivity Dilemma: Roadblock to Innovation in the Automobile Industry,* Baltimore: Johns Hopkins University Press.

Abramovitz, M., 1956, "Resources and Output Trends in the United States since 1870," *American Economic Review,* vol. 46, no. 2, May, pp. 5–23.

Afriat, S. N., 1972, "Efficiency Estimation of Production Functions," *International Economic Review,* vol. 13, no. 3, October, pp. 568–98.

Aigner, D., and S. Chu, 1968, "On Estimating the Industry Production Function," *American Economic Review,* vol. 58, no. 4, September, pp. 826–39.

Baker Kenneth R., 1974, *Introduction to Sequencing and Scheduling,* New York: John Wiley & Sons.

Beal, Edwin F., E. D. Wickersham, and P. Kienast, 1972, *The Practice of Collective Bargaining,* 4th ed., Homewood, Ill.: Richard D. Irwin.

Berndt, Ernst R., and David O. Wood, 1979, "Engineering and Economic Interpretations of Energy-Capital Complementarity," *American Economic Review,* vol. 69, no. 3, June, pp 342–54.

Berndt, Ernst R., and Dale W. Jorgenson, 1978, "How Energy, and Its Cost Enter the Productivity Equation," *IEEE Spectrum,* vol. 15, no. 10, October, pp. 50–52.

Brennan, Donald P., 1978, "Management—Assessing Its Role in Improvement of Productivity," *Paper Trade Journal,* December 1–15, pp. 47–49.

Christensen, Laurits R., Dale W. Jorgenson, and L. J. Lau, 1973, "Transcendental Logarithmic Production Frontiers," *Review of Economics and Statistics,* vol. 55, no. 1, February, pp. 28–45.

_____, 1971, "Conjugate Duality and the Transcendental Logarithmic Production Function," *Econometrica,* vol. 39, no. 4, July, pp. 255–56.

Christensen, Laurits R., and Dale W. Jorgenson, 1970, "U.S. Real Product and Real Factor Input, 1929–1967," *Review of Income and Wealth,* series 16, no. 1, March, pp. 19–50.

_____, 1969, "Measurement of U.S. Real Capital Input, 1927–1967," *Review of Income and Wealth,* series 15, no. 4, December, pp. 293–320.

Clark, Peter K., 1979, "Issues in the Analysis of Capital Formation and Productivity Growth," *Brookings Papers on Economic Activity,* vol. 2, pp. 423–31.

_____, 1978, "Capital Formation and the Recent Productivity Slowdown," *Journal of Finance,* vol. 33, June, pp. 965–75.

Council of Economic Advisers, 1980, Annual Report, in *Economic Report of the President,* Washington, D.C.: U.S. Government Printing Office.

_____, 1979, Annual Report, in *Economic Report of the President,* Washington, D.C.: U.S. Government Printing Office.

Craig, Charles E., and R. Clark Harris, 1973, "Total Productivity Measurement at the Firm Level," *Sloan Management Review,* vol. 14, no. 3, pp. 13–29.

Denison, Edward F., 1979a, *Accounting for Slower Economic Growth: The U.S. in the 70's,* Washington, D.C.: Brookings.

_____, 1979b, "Explanation of Declining Productivity Growth," *Survey of Current Business,* vol. 59, no. 8, August, Part 2, pp. 1–24.

_____, 1972, "Final Comments," *Survey of Current Business,* vol. 52, no. 5, May, Part 2, pp. 95–110.

_____, 1969, "Some Major Issues in Productivity Analysis: An Examination of Estimates by Jorgenson and Griliches," *Survey of Current Business,* vol. 49, no. 5, May, Part 2, pp. 1–27.

_____, 1962, *Sources of Economic Growth in the U.S. and the Alternatives before Us,* Supplementary Paper 13, Washington, D.C.: Committee for Economic Development.

Dhrymes, Phoebus J., 1963, "A Comparison of Productivity Behavior in Manufacturing and Service Industries," *Review of Economics and Statistics,* vol. 45, no. 1, pp. 64–69.

Eilon, Samuel, Bela Gold, and Judith Soesan, 1976, *Applied Productivity Analysis for Industry,* Oxford: Pergamon Press.

Erdilek, Asim, 1977, "Productivity, Technological Change, and Input-Output Analysis," in *Research, Technological Change, and Economic Analysis,* edited by Bela Gold, Lexington, Mass.: Lexington Books.

Fabricant, Solomon, 1977, "Perspective on the Capital Requirements Question," in *Capital for Productivity and Jobs,* edited by Eli Shapiro and William L. White, Englewood Cliffs, N.J.: Prentice-Hall, pp. 27–49.

_____, 1969, *A Primer on Productivity,* New York: Random House.

_____, 1959, *Basic Facts on Productivity Change,* Occasional Paper 63, New York: National Bureau of Economic Research.

Farnsworth, R. A., 1975, *Productivity and the Law,* Westmead: Saxon House; Lexington, Mass.: Lexington Books.

Farrell, M., 1957, "The Measurement of Productive Efficiency," *Journal of the Royal Statistical Society,* series A, vol. 120, Part 3, 1957, pp. 253–90.

Finger, Nachum, 1971, *The Impact of Government Subsidies on Industrial Management,* New York: Praeger Publishers.

Fraiman, Nelson M., 1978, "Growth of Administrative Employment and Output in U.S. Steel Industry," *Journal of Economic Issues,* vol. 12, no. 2, June.

Francis, Richard L., and John A. White, 1974, *Facility Layout and Location,* Englewood Cliffs, N.J.: Prentice-Hall.

Freeman, JoAnne H., and James V. Jucker, 1981, "Comparing the Productivity of Traditional and Innovative Work Organizations," in *Productivity Analysis at the Organizational Level,* edited by N. R. Adam and A. Dogramaci, Boston: Martinus Nijhoff Publishing.

Georgopoulos, Basil S., Gerald M. Mahoney, and Nyle W. Jones, 1957, "A Path-Goal Approach to Productivity," *Journal of Applied Psychology,* vol. 41, pp. 345–53.

Gitlow, Abraham L., 1964, *The National Wage Policy: Antecedents and Application,* New York: New York University Press.

Glaser, Edward M., 1976, *Productivity Gains through Worklife Improvements,* New York: Harcourt Brace Jovanovich.

Gold, Bela, 1979, *Productivity, Technology and Capital,* Lexington, Mass.: Lexington Books.

_____, 1977, *Research, Technological Change and Economic Analysis,* Lexington, Mass.: Lexington Books.

_____, 1976, "A Framework for Productivity Analysis," in Eilon, Gold, and Soesan (1976).

_____, 1975, *Technological Change: Economics, Management and Environment,* Oxford: Pergamon Press.

_____, 1973, "Technology, Productivity and Economic Analysis," *Omega, The International Journal of Management Science,* vol. 1, no. 1, February, pp. 5–24.

_____, 1971, *Explorations in Managerial Economics: Productivity, Costs, Technology and Growth,* London: Macmillan; New York: Basic Books.

_____, 1964, "Economic Effects of Technological Innovations," *Management Science,* vol. 11, no. 1, September, pp. 105–34.

_____, 1955, *Foundations of Productivity Analysis,* Pittsburgh: University of Pittsburgh Press.

Grant, Eugene L., and Richard S. Leavenworth, 1972, *Statistical Quality Control,* New York: McGraw-Hill.

Grayson, C. Jackson, Jr., 1978, "Our Lagging Productivity: Too High a Price to Pay," *Finance Magazine,* July/August, pp. 5–7.

Greenberg, Leon, 1973, *A Practical Guide to Productivity Measurement,* Washington D.C.: Bureau of National Affairs.

Greenman, Russell L., and Eric J. Schmertz, 1979, *Personnel Administration and the Law,* 2nd ed., Washington D.C.: Bureau of National Affairs.

Griliches, Zvi, 1979, "Issues in Assessing the Contribution of Research and Development to Productivity Growth," *Bell Journal of Economics,* vol. 10, no. 1, Spring, pp. 92–116.

Griliches, Zvi, and Dale W. Jorgenson, 1966, "Sources of Measured Productivity Change: Capital Input," *American Economic Review,* vol. 56, no. 2, May, pp. 50–61.

Harriss, C. Lowell, 1975, *Inflation,* New York: Praeger Publishers.

Hines, William W., 1976, "Guidelines for Implementing Productivity Measurement," *Industrial Engineering,* June, pp. 40–43.

Hudson, Edward A., and Dale W. Jorgenson, 1978, "Energy Prices and the U.S. Economy, 1972–1976," *Natural Resources Journal,* vol. 18, no. 4, October.

Hulten, Charles R., 1979, "On the Importance of Productivity Change," *American Economic Review,* vol. 69, no. 1, March, pp. 126–36.

Johansen, Leif, 1972, *Production Functions,* Amsterdam: North-Holland Publishing.

———, 1961, "A Method for Separating the Effects of Capital Accumulation and Shift in Production Functions upon Growth in Labor Productivity," *Economic Journal,* vol. 71, December, pp. 775–82.

Johnson, Richard A., William T. Newell, and Roger C. Vergin, 1974, *Production and Operations Management,* Boston: Houghton Mifflin.

Jorgenson, Dale W., 1979a, "Energy and the Future U.S. Economy," *Wharton Magazine,* vol. 3, no. 4, Summer, pp. 15–21.

———, 1979b, "Accounting for Capital," in *Capital, Efficiency and Growth,* edited by George M. von Furstenberg, Cambridge, Mass.: Ballinger Publishing.

Jorgenson, Dale W., and L. J. Lau, 1981, *Transcendental Logarithmic Production Functions,* Amsterdam: North-Holland Publishing.

Jorgenson, Dale W., and Z. Griliches, 1972a, "Issues in Growth Accounting: Final Reply," *Survey of Current Business,* vol. 52, no. 5, May, Part 2, p. 111.

———, 1972b, "Issues in Growth Accounting: A Reply to Edward F. Denison," *Survey of Current Business,* vol. 52, no. 5, May, Part 2, pp. 65–94.

———, 1967, "The Explanation of Productivity Change," *Review of Economic Studies,* vol. 34, no. 99, pp. 249–83.

Jorgenson, Dale W., J. J. McCall, and R. Radner, 1967, *Optimal Replacement Policy,* Chicago: Rand McNally; Amsterdam: North-Holland Publishing.

Katzell, Raymond A., Penney Bienstock, and Paul H. Faerstein, 1977, *A Guide to Worker Productivity Experiments in the United States, 1971–1975,* New York: New York University Press.

Kendrick, John W., 1977, *Understanding Productivity,* Baltimore: Johns Hopkins University Press.

———, 1973, *Postwar Productivity Trends in the U.S., 1948-1969,* New York: National Bureau of Economic Research.

———, 1961, *Productivity Trends in the U.S.,* Princeton, N.J.: Princeton University Press.

———, 1956, "Productivity Trends: Capital and Labor," *Review of Economics and Statistics,* vol. 38, no. 3, August, pp. 248-57.

Kendrick, John W., and Daniel Creamer, 1965, *Measuring Company Productivity,* Conference Board Studies in Business Economics, no. 89, New York: National Industrial Conference Board.

Kimberly, J. R., and W. R. Nielsen, 1975, "Organization Development and Change in Organizational Performance," *Administrative Science Quarterly,* vol. 20, no. 2, June, pp. 191-206.

King, A. S., 1974, "Expectation Effects in Organizational Change," *Administrative Science Quarterly,* vol. 19, no. 2, June, pp. 221-30.

Kuznets, Simon, 1966, *Modern Economic Growth,* New Haven, Conn.: Yale University Press.

Leontief, Wassily W., 1966, *Input Output Economics,* New York: Oxford University Press.

———, 1951, *The Structure of American Economy, 1919-1939,* New York: Oxford University Press.

Leontief, Wassily W., et al., 1977, *The Future of World Economy,* New York: Oxford University Press.

McConnell, Campbell, R., 1979, "Why Is U.S. Productivity Slowing Down?" *Harvard Business Review,* March-April, pp. 16-25.

Malkiel, Burton G., 1979, "Productivity—The Problem behind the Headlines," *Harvard Business Review,* May-June, pp. 17-27.

Mansfield, Edwin, 1971, *Technological Change,* 2nd ed., New York: W. W. Norton.

———, 1968, *Industrial Research and Technological Innovation; An Econometric Analysis,* New York: W. W. Norton.

Mansfield, Edwin, et al., 1977, *The Production and Application of New Industrial Technology,* New York: W. W. Norton.

Melman, Seymour, 1974, *The Permanent War Economy,* New York: Simon & Schuster.

———, 1971, "Managerial versus Cooperative Decision Making in Israel," *Studies in Comparative International Development,* vol. 6, no. 3, 1970-71, Rutgers University; Sage Publications.

———, 1965, *Our Depleted Society,* New York: Dell Books.

———, 1958, *Decision Making and Productivity,* New York: John Wiley & Sons.

———, 1956, Dynamic Factors in Industrial Productivity, New York: John Wiley & Sons.

Moon, I. Douglas, 1981, "Technological Change and Productivity in Input-Output Analysis and the Potential of Sectoral Optimization Models," in *Aggregate and*

Industry-Level Productivity Analyses, edited by A. Dogramaci and N. R. Adam, Boston: Martinus Nijhoff Publishing.

Mundel, Marvin E., 1978, *Motion and Time Study,* 5th ed., Englewood Cliffs, N.J.: Prentice-Hall.

Muther, Richard, 1973, Systematic Layout Planning, 2nd ed., Boston: Cahners Books.

Nadiri, M. Ishaq, 1979, "Contributions and Determinants of Research and Development Expenditures in the U.S. Manufacturing Industries," Working Paper No. 360, June, New York: National Bureau of Economic Research.

_____, 1970, "Some Approaches to the Theory and Measurement of Total Factor Productivity," *Journal of Economic Literature,* vol. 8, no. 4, December, pp. 1137-77.

Nadiri, M. Ishaq, and M. A. Schankerman, 1979, "The Structure of Production, Technological Change, and the Rate of Growth of Total Factor Productivity in the Bell System," Working Paper No. 358, June, New York: National Bureau of Economic Research.

National Center for Productivity and Quality of Working Life, 1978, *Productivity in the Changing World of the 1980's,* Washington, D.C.: U.S. Government Printing Office.

New York Stock Exchange, 1979, *Reaching a Higher Standard of Living,* Office of Economic Research, January.

Norsworthy, J. R., and M. J. Harper, 1981, "The Role of Capital Formation in the Recent Slowdown in Productivity Growth," in *Aggregate and Industry-Level Productivity Analyses,* edited by A. Dogramaci and N. R. Adam, Boston: Martinus Nijhoff Publishing.

Pratten, C. F., 1976*a,* "Labour Productivity Differentials within International Companies," University of Cambridge, Department of Applied Economics, Occasional Papers, no. 50, Cambridge: Cambridge University Press,

_____, 1976*b,* "A Comparison of the Performance of Swedish and U.K. Companies," University of Cambridge, Department of Applied Economics, Occasional Papers, no. 47, Cambridge: Cambridge University Press.

Rees, Albert, 1979, "Improving the Concepts and Techniques of Productivity Measurement," *Monthly Labor Review,* vol. 102, no. 9, September, pp. 23-27.

Riggs, James L., 1980, "One Strike on Productivity," *Industrial Engineering,* June and July.

_____, 1979, "Wa: Personnel Factor of Japanese Productivity," *Industrial Engineering,* vol. 11, no. 4, April.

_____, 1978, "Improved Productivity Needs Leadership—Yours," *Industrial Engineering,* vol. 10, no. 11, November, pp. 45-49.

_____, 1972, *Production Systems,* New York: John Wiley & Sons.

Salter, W. E. G., 1966, *Productivity and Technical Change,* 2nd ed., London: Cambridge University Press.

Samuelson, Paul A., 1973, *Economics,* 9th ed., New York: McGraw-Hill.

Sato, Kazuo, 1981, "Theoretical Issues in Production Accounting," in *Asian Income and Wealth,* vol. 2, edited by K. Ohkawa, Tokyo: University of Tokyo Press.

_____, 1976, "The Ideal Log Change Index Number," *Review of Economics and Statistics,* vol. 58, May, pp. 223–28.

Schmidt, Peter, and C. A. Knox Lovell, 1979, "Estimating Technical and Allocative in Efficiency Relative to Stochastic Production and Cost Frontiers," *Journal of Econometrics,* vol. 9, no. 3, February, pp. 343–66.

Solow, R. M., 1957, "Technical Change and the Aggregate Production Function," *Review of Economics and Statistics,* vol. 39, no. 3, August, pp. 312–20.

Starr, Martin K., 1973, "Productivity Is the U.S.A.'s Problem," *California Management Review,* vol. 16, no. 2, Winter, pp. 32–36.

_____, 1978, *Operations Management,* Englewood Cliffs, N.J.: Prentice-Hall.

Sutermeister, Robert A., 1976. *People and Productivity,* New York: McGraw-Hill.

Tatom, John A., 1979, "The Productivity Problem," *Review of Federal Reserve Bank of St. Louis,* September, pp. 3–16.

Terleckyj, Nestor, 1974, *Effects of R&D on the Productivity Growth of Industries: An Exploratory Study,* Report No. 140, December, Washington D.C.: National Planning Association.

United Nations, 1973, *Input-Output Tables and Analysis,* Department of Economics and Social Affairs Statistical Office, Studies in Methods, series F, no. 14, New York: United Nations.

U.S. Department of Commerce, 1979, *International Economic Indicators,* vol. 5, no. 4, December.

Wild, Ray, 1972, *Mass-Production Management,* London: John Wiley & Sons.

Work in America, 1973, Report of a Special Task Force to the Secretary of Health Education and Welfare, Cambridge, Mass.: MIT Press.

2 ISSUES IN PRODUCTIVITY MEASUREMENT AND ANALYSIS

Solomon Fabricant

2.1. INTRODUCTION

Every live subject—by definition—poses issues on which people differ. Judged by this criterion, the subject of productivity is very much alive these days.

In saying this, I have in mind not only the many scientific studies and conferences being devoted to productivity or to data essential in dealing with it.[1] There are also the innumerable current uses being made of productivity measurements and theories in arguments over the direction and implementation of policies to speed up economic growth, meet competition in international markets, dampen the rate of inflation, and reach a better physical and social environment, to cite the outstanding examples.

Indeed, the issues that might be put together from all this mount up to a sizable number, and they are complicated. During 1969–1972 anyone who tried to thread his way through the fine print or even just the primer type of the long exchanges on productivity measurement between Denison, on the one side, and Jorgenson and Griliches, on the other, will recall the effort he had to make; and in that controversy, issues of analysis and policy were more implied than expressed.[2]

But the present purpose will be served if the list of issues is kept short—shorter, certainly, than the long research agenda I felt obliged to offer in 1973 (see Fabricant, 1974).[3] In other respects, however, it will not be as different as one might hope to see after the lapse of six years. True, in our subject, as in other areas of human concern, the issues change over time as progress is made in understanding the subject. Some issues amenable to empirical and logical testing do get settled or put aside when found to be of minor importance. However, our scientific progress has been slow. Most of the old issues, whether classified under one or more of the conventional headings of concept, measurement, analysis, and policy, are still with us. What has mainly been changed is the emphasis put upon particular issues. In the social sciences, to a much greater extent than in other sciences, the issues attracting attention reflect the current problems and purposes of society; in an evolving world, these problems change, as do the values people attach to the costs and benefits involved. On this occasion, then, I have drawn my examples from the issues to which recent developments call, or recall, our attention.

2.2. THE SLOWDOWN OF
U.S. PRODUCTIVITY GROWTH

Dominant among the above developments is the slowdown in productivity growth, sharply evident in 1973. But there have been other developments, including general price inflation; the drastic jump in the relative price of petroleum in 1973; the accelerated movement of women into the labor force; the continued rise in the relative importance of the health industry and other service industries, including government, and the even greater rise in their costs; and the greatly increased emphasis placed on the quality of the environment, the quality of working life, and the protection of workers and consumers against risks in these and other respects. These developments, the reader will recognize, are not independent of one another. It will be sufficient, therefore, to concentrate on the productivity-growth slowdown and to bring the others in as they bear on the issues raised by the slowdown. It should be understood also that I take my job to be that of posing the issues, not resolving them. Their resolution is a task for many hands, working with many more data than are now available.

The slowdown in productivity growth after 1973 is evident in all the available measures of productivity, despite differences in their concepts, coverage, and construction.

The slowdown can be seen very clearly in the indexes of what most people think of as productivity—namely, output per worker-hour or labor productivity. Most widely known is the Bureau of Labor Statistics index of output per worker-hour in the private business sector, reported in the BLS's quarterly press releases on productivity and costs and then in many news media the next day. Up to 1973, this measure of productivity rose between peak years of cyclical activity at average annual rates fluctuating between 2.3 and 3.6 percent, with the average for 1948–1973 equal to 3.1 (Fabricant, 1979, Table 6). But then, between the peak year 1973 and 1978 (which falls short of being a peak year), the average annual rate fell off to 0.9 percent. A broader labor productivity index—for the entire economy, covering government and other nonbusiness sectors as well as private business—was recently published for selected periods through 1977 (Council of Economic Advisers, 1979, Table 16). This index rose at an average annual rate of 2.6 percent between 1950 and 1965, 1.9 percent between 1965 and 1973, and only 1.1 percent between 1973 and 1977; and there is every indication that the rise was less than 1 percent between 1977 and 1978.

The slowdown in productivity growth after 1973 is clear also in the various private estimates of "total factor," or "multifactor" productivity that are available to a recent year. These, as their designation indicates, compare output, not with worker-hours alone, but with some more or less complete measure of total factor input, including tangible capital as well as labor input.[4] Specifically, Denison's estimate of the rate of change per annum in "output per unit of labor and capital in the nonresidential business sector" dropped to a negative 0.7 percent during 1973–1976, from 1.6 percent for 1969–1973 or 2.1 percent for the whole of the preceding postwar period, 1948–1973 (Denison, 1978a). Kendrick's latest estimates of growth in "real gross product per unit of total factor input in the domestic business economy" dropped to 0.7 percent for 1973–1977, from 1.6 percent for 1969–1973 and 2.7 percent for 1948–1973 (Kendrick, 1979). The estimates by Christensen and his collaborators of change in "gross private domestic product (including the product yielded by household capital) per unit of total factor input" declined to 0.0 percent for 1973–1977, from 1.2 percent for 1969–1973 and 1.3 percent for 1948–1973 (Christensen, Cummings, and Jorgenson, 1978; Christensen and Jorgenson, 1979). None of these indexes of total factor productivity is available through 1978, but we can be sure here too that developments since 1976 or 1977 would not alter our conclusion.

The slowdown shocked us out of any complacency we may have felt regarding our understanding of productivity and productivity change. Trend rates of growth of productivity, whether defined as labor or as total factor productivity, were not nearly as low before 1973 (at least back to 1890) as the rate for 1973–1978, except possibly between the years bounding the depressions of 1892–1895, 1907–1910, and 1929–1937, and the war years 1913–1920 (Bureau of Economic Analysis, 1973; Fabricant, 1979, Table 7.)

Three more or less distinct questions arose, and since the answers varied, three issues, or groups of issues, were posed.

2.3. MEASUREMENT PROBLEMS

First, doubts grew about the validity of the statistics. We became less sure than we had been about our indexes of productivity. Some economists even wondered whether the slowdown was merely an artifact, reflecting a deterioration in the quality of the statistics used to construct the productivity measures.

Now, it so happens that a labor-productivity-growth slowdown occurred also in other industrial countries (Daly and Neef, 1978). According to indexes available for manufacturing, between 1973 and 1977 the average rate of increase in output per worker-hour in Canada, Japan, and eight European countries was less than it had been during 1960–1973 in every case but one. Indeed, the decline in most foreign rates was greater than the decline had been in the United States.[5] But the slowdown abroad provides only limited assurance of the validity of our own indexes, for the sources of doubt about the quality of the currently underlying statistics are much the same abroad as they are here.

Questions about the validity of the statistics used in measuring the output and input that we compare in deriving our productivity indexes are not new. An example of the questions that have troubled us before and continue to trouble us today concerns the measure of government output. It is assumed to parallel government employment (except for an adjustment for change in the average educational level of government workers); thus it fails to show any increases in government output per worker-hour that may result from the large and increasing volume of services provided by governmentally owned tangible capital and from improvement in the efficiency with which government managers use the labor and capital employed in government activities. This is a major reason why the BLS, among others, prefers to confine its labor productivity measure to the private business sector, and why the productivity index for the economy as a whole (the index cited by the Council of Economic Advisers in the *Economic Report of the President,* 1979) has grown less rapidly than the productivity index for the private business sector.

But there are similar questions about the productivity indexes of some industries in the private business sector. And there are plenty of other questions as well, as the report of the National Research Council's Panel on Productivity Statistics will show. It is not easy to answer these questions. Even when there is general agreement on the existence of a bias and on its direction—which is not always the case—there are usually differences of opinion on how important the bias is, and there is still less agreement on the degree to which the bias grew or diminished and thus affected the rate of retardation, as well as the average slope of the line describing the trend of productivity.

One such question, for example, concerns the degree of quality improvement in producers' and consumers' equipment and in medical and other health services that is not captured by the available statistics. It is very difficult to measure or even to define quality change, as Griliches and other economists have been telling us (Griliches, 1971; Lancaster, 1977) and as economists and statisticians in the BLS know by hard experience, confronted as they are with the task of writing specifications for products changing as rapidly as automobiles have been in this age of strong antipollution policy. Indeed not every expert is willing to admit that "uncaptured" quality change has been significant on net balance or that anyone can be sure whether it has been or not. This being the case, we can expect to find wide differences of opinion regarding the effect of change in the rate of quality change on the retardation in the growth rate witnessed after (or before) 1973.

Some of the questions about biases in the statistics have been put in terms of the *shift effect* resulting from the continuing relative increase of employment in the service industries. If the level of service productivity is understated relative to the level in the nonservice industries, for reasons similar to those affecting the government productivity measures (as is most probably the case), such a shift effect would result.[6] This could certainly help to explain both a downward bias in the average rate of increase in productivity and a degree of retardation in this rate. But here, too, the importance of the shift effect is difficult to determine with the rather gross data currently available. I have the impression, after some struggle with the figures, that the shift effect has not been important in accounting for retardation in the rate of productivity growth either before or after 1973—which does not mean that it has been altogether negligible—but this is an opinion with which others may differ.

Another possibility of bias originates in the development—abroad as well as here—of rapid inflation and the rather inept efforts of government to deal with it. As a result, the price statistics we (and other countries) use to deflate current values in order to get at real output and input are affected. For example, sales of goods made to order will generally be at prices prevailing at the time the order is placed. If value of shipments is deflated by the BLS by market prices prevailing at the time of shipment, as they often are, "measured" real output will tend to be biased downward in an era of inflation. This understatement will not affect the rates of change when inflation is at a steady pace. But this is seldom the case. When inflation accelerates, as it did in the 1960s and early 1970s, the rate of change of real output will be understated, and so will the rate of change of productivity. The net effect during 1973–1978, taking account of slowdowns as well as spurts in the rate of inflation and of the widening recourse to escalator clauses in order contracts, is unclear, however. Some net retarding influence may exist, but whether in fact and by how much are open to question.[7] Further complications in an era of inflation arise from the introduction of price guidelines and the like. Businessmen may find it advisable to keep list prices up even when their actual prices have been reduced. On the other hand, there is also a tendency to keep list prices down when actual prices are raised. Direct evidence on the difference between list and realized prices is scanty, however, and more would be costly to obtain, as Stigler and Kindahl (1970) learned a decade ago.

A clue to the quantitative effect of inflation on the productivity indexes is provided by the rather unusual differences noticeable between the recent behavior of real GNP originating in manufacturing and the industrial production index that is published by the Federal Reserve Board and based on physical volume data. Between 1973 and 1978 real GNP originating in manufacturing (used in calculating the BLS's index of productivity) rose at the average annual rate of 1.8 percent, while the Fed's index of manufacturing production rose at the higher rate of 2.3 percent. A similar difference appeared during the Korean inflation. In contrast, during the earlier part of the 1960s when inflation was slight, the difference was negligible. But here, too, there remains some considerable uncertainty. The concepts, as well as the sources of the two indexes, differ; they need not always or necessarily run parallel to one another; and the Fed's index also has its critics.[8] An analysis more elaborate than any done so far—requiring more data than are now available—is needed to resolve the issue.[9]

2.4. TIMING OF THE SLOWDOWN

Second, accepting the productivity statistics as sufficiently reliable, there are doubts as to just when the slowdown began, as I have already hinted. Was the slowdown after 1973 in fact the continuation and also aggravation of a trend noticeable earlier?

The figures cited earlier do provide signs of retardation prior to 1973. In fact, a curvilinear (logarithmic parabola) trend line I fitted to the BLS series on output per worker-hour in the private business sector covering the period 1948–1973 yields a statistically significant rate of retardation of 0.04 percentage points per year (Fabricant, 1978, Chart 3). So low a rate of retardation may not seem like much, but it cumulates; it meant a drop in the average annual rate of productivity growth from 3.4 percent around 1948 to 2.4 percent around 1973. Then, during the business recession after 1973, an unusually sharp and sustained decline occurred in the productivity level. For the first time since 1947 when the BLS's quarterly record of productivity change began, there was an absolute decline in productivity during as many as seven consecutive quarters. The business recovery that began in 1975 brought the productivity level back up to and then above the 1973 peak, but the rise to 1978 was insufficient to carry the productivity level up to the point reached by the long-term trend line (allowing, of course, for a continuation of the secular rate of retardation after 1973). In effect, the picture seems to be one of gradual retardation prior to 1973, followed by a sharply aggravated increase—perhaps temporary—in the rate of retardation after 1973.

In the recent *Economic Report of the President* referred to above (Council of Economic Advisers, 1979, pp. 72–73), the Council of Economic Advisers (CEA) considered this picture in the course of their discussion of the trend underlying the growth of potential national output over the 1973–1978 period. The council presented two different interpretations of the productivity trend after 1973. The "optimistic view," as they put it, holds that the sharp declines, particularly between 1973 and 1974 and to a lesser extent in 1977–78, resulted from "nonrecurring factors affecting the level of productivity, after which the long-term trend of productivity growth resumed its earlier pace," or may be expected to resume it after 1978. The "pessimistic view" holds that the 1973–74 period was not extraordinary, that the "long-term productivity growth began to slow substantially after the mid-1960's, although unexpectedly favorable developments in late 1972 and in early 1973 disguised the fact. The poor average performance of productivity since early 1973 reflects that slowdown, and the particularly disappointing episodes in 1973–74 and 1977–78 are fluctuations around a greatly reduced long-term trend." As might be expected, the CEA finally concluded—or more accurately assumed—that the actual trend probably falls between the two extremes: some earlier retardation already visible before 1973 and some unusual developments since 1973, a view similar to the one I have already expressed.

But what unusual developments? And what of the factors involved in the earlier retardation? This brings us to our third set of questions: What can explain the changes, and particularly the recent retardation, in the rate of productivity growth?

2.5. ACCOUNTING FOR THE SLOWDOWN

Many of us had begun to believe that we understood at least the proximate sources of change in productivity. Thus, to use Denison's classification and estimates of the sources of change in labor productivity (Denison, 1974, 1978*b*), the gradual retardation in productivity growth between 1948 and 1973 could be readily "explained." First, there was a tendency for capital per worker-hour to grow at a retarded rate; second, the age-sex composition of the labor force shifted from a positive contribution during 1948–1953 to a negative contribution by 1969–1973, as the proportion of women in the labor force accelerated; third, a falling off—especially during 1969–1973—occurred in the rate of improvement in resource allocation resulting from the shift of workers from farm and nonfarm self-employment to better paying occupations elsewhere; and fourth, there was a somewhat accelerated rise in the costs associated with changes in the institutional and human environment. Of all the sources distinguished in Denison's studies of the sources of economic growth, only the improvement in the quality of education was at its high point during 1969–1973. The net outcome of changes in these measured sources was sufficient to account for the entire drop between 1948 and 1973 in the rate of growth of labor productivity.

Admittedly, we were left, in the form of a residual, with a substantial chunk—almost half—of growth in productivity unaccounted for. But this residual—entitled "advances in knowledge and not elsewhere classified"—was fairly stable, and it was almost taken for granted that it reflected mostly (if not entirely) the contribution of advances in knowledge. This presumption conformed to the habit economists had of designating shifts in the production function—measured by the residual—as technical or technological change. But then came the slowdown after 1973, not only in the United States but elsewhere, and the situation was quite different from what it had been before 1973.

Trying to explain the slowdown and to understand what its causes could foretell about the future, for we dared no longer simply extrapolate the past trend, made us more keenly aware than ever of how little we really knew about sources of productivity change.

Some of the measured factors that had contributed to the pre-1973 retardation were still operating after 1973, if we may judge from estimates running through 1976 or 1977. Tangible capital per worker-hour again rose less rapidly than before. This source therefore tended to lower the rate of growth of labor productivity. Also pushing in a negative direction were a further decline in the contribution of improved resource allocation and a sharp increase in the costs incurred in improving the physical and human environment. With output rising less rapidly after 1973 than before, there was less benefit from increase in economies of scale; the contribution of this source also declined. On the other hand, there was a higher rate of improvement in the quality of labor, due mainly to acceleration in the positive contribution of education. The net of all this was negligible and could not even begin to account for the sharp decline in labor productivity (or total factor productivity) after 1973. A very appreciable negative contribution from the residual was indicated.

Yet it hardly seemed possible to point a finger at the contribution of advances in knowledge as the dominant factor in the residual, as had been the custom. The stock of knowledge is massive; its growth has great momentum. Could the decline after 1967 in the gross investment made in knowledge—measured by expenditures on R&D—cause the rate of advance in the stock and services of knowledge to decline nearly as much as the residual suggested was necessary?[10]

I recall vividly the hearing before the Joint Economic Committee at which Denison (1978a, p. 490) described the drop in the rate of change in productivity after 1973.[11] He went on to explain the drop in terms of his usual classification along the lines already indicated and ended up with a residual, the contribution of which had declined from 1.6 percentage points during 1969–1973 to a negative 0.7 percentage points during 1973–1976 —that is, by the extraordinary amount of 2.3 percentage points. He then asked himself, why the sudden change? Looking up, he tossed his papers upon the table and said, "I am going to stop here, because I don't know why."

Contrast Denison's figures and attitude with Kendrick's. In the memorandum Kendrick prepared for the report by the N.Y. Stock Exchange cited above (Kendrick, 1979), he felt able and willing to provide a much fuller and more detailed set of estimates of the sources of change in productivity than had Denison. (These covered the change in the rate of growth of labor productivity between 1966–1973 and 1973–1977, with 1977 marked "preliminary".) In Kendrick's table, decline in the contributions of advances in knowledge—estimated directly from R&D expenditures, assumed obsolescence rates, and other data, rather than as a residual—amounted to only 0.2 percentage points. The residual he did have, much smaller than Denison's and entitled "actual potential efficiency and not elsewhere classified," showed a modest increase of 0.2 percentage points in its contribution.

Clearly, there are wide differences revealed here. Not everyone agrees on what can and what cannot be considered as measurable proximate sources of change in productivity, at least not now and for the present purpose; and not all agree on how the measurable sources should be measured and how well they are measured.

The issues concern not only the adequacy of the basic statistical data and the point at which estimation becomes too uncertain to warrant offering the resulting measurements to the public rather than reserving them for professional discussion; the issues arise also over the adequacy of the analysis, including the economic and econometric assumptions made explicitly or implicitly in establishing the cause-and-effect connection between a source and a consequent change in productivity.

We know, for example, that the various measures of sources of change in productivity are interrelated; their separate contributions are therefore not easy to distinguish. Thus, doubling the rate of increase in tangible capital, were the rates of increase in other inputs to remain constant, would not double tangible capital's contribution because of diminishing returns as the proportion of capital to the other inputs increased. But estimation of the increase depends on the shape of the production function fitted to the data, as well as the data used. On these, opinions—and the results obtained—can differ widely.

Also, to some extent, inputs complement one another. Technological change, to a significant degree, must be embodied in tangible capital if it is to be put to use in production. The contribution of technology then depends in part on the rate of increase in tangible capital, as well as on its own rate of increase. But how much it depends is also a subject of contention, as indicated in the discussion at the 1977 Christmas meetings of the Social Science Associations on the productivity growth slowdown.[12]

More can be said also about the residual, as Denison estimated it after allowing, among other things, for the diversion of capital investment to meet the accelerated changes in regulations to improve the institutional and human environment already mentioned (Denison, 1978b). Prior to 1973, this factor was minor, causing a reduction of less than 0.1 percentage points per annum in the rate of productivity growth. After 1973 (measured to 1976), the reduction was 0.4 percentage points per annum. But this is not the whole story of the effect of Occupational Safety and Health Administration (OSHA) regulations and other regulatory legislation on productivity. In addition to diverting investment to protect better the physical environment and safety and health of workers, in recent years there has been also a substantial degree of diversion of management's time in order to learn what the regulations mean, how and when the regulations may be expected to change, and how to adjust to them now and in the future; in addition, R&D personnel have been diverted to cope with the technical problems raised. These factors are among the residual.

Another development tending in the same direction is the cartel-induced rise in the price of petroleum in 1973 and since then. In this case also, investment of funds and time have had (and will have) to be devoted to learning how to adjust to the radically new set of relative cost prices and then to making the adjustment. The task has not been made easier with business-men's having to worry about the complicated energy policies that have come and will continue to come out of Washington. Here, also, is a factor, contributing to the slowdown, that is hidden within the residual.

The high and unsteady rate of inflation, as I have already noted, may have played a part in overstating the extent of the slowdown. But along with the erratic governmental efforts to deal with inflation, it has also played a role in contributing to the slowdown of productivity by inhibiting capital formation, as well as in other ways reflected in the "n.e.c." part of the residual. In many industries, inflation and guidelines have troubled labor-management relations and negotiations and aggravated the uncertainties that confront businessmen; moreover, inflation has been raising the effec-tive income tax rate and confusing people trying to make sense of conven-tional accounting statements when planning their investments.

Also left unspecified in the residual, to give still another example, are the fluctuations in the federal government's support of R&D, which could hardly have failed to lower the efficiency with which research and develop-ent, and especially basic research, are planned and carried out.

How important these factors really are in dampening incentives to raise productivity and thus accounting for the slowdown is a matter of contro-versy. But it hardly seems sensible to ignore them or to presume that their effects—en masse—have been negligible.

All in all, then, we have some distance to go to determine, or to deter-mine more accurately, the reasons for the recent slowdown and the retarda-tion that preceded it. And it is fair to say that there is much to do also to im-prove our knowledge of the factors that account for the persistently upward long-term trend of productivity.

2.6. FINAL REMARKS

I do not suppose that I need say any more to persuade the reader that many issues in productivity measurement and analysis—not to mention pol-icy—require attention. Let me add only that in dwelling on the issues that separate us, I do not mean to belittle the knowledge we already have and share in common. Our progress has been slow, but we do know more today than we did some years ago—certainly much more than we knew when the first Conference on Productivity was held in Washington in 1946.[13]

NOTES

1. For instance: the papers and comments on them presented at meetings of the Conference on Research in Income and Wealth entitled "New Developments in Productivity Measurement," 1975, "The Measurement of Capital," 1976 (see Kendrick and Vaccara, 1980; Usher, 1980), and "The National Income and Product Accounts of the United States," 1979; the report of the National Research Council on productivity statistics (see Panel on Productivity Statistics, 1979); the conferences of the International Association for Research in Income and Wealth, one held in New York in 1978 and another in Austria in 1979, the papers of which are or will be published in the *Review of Income and Wealth;* and the conference sponsored by the National Science Foundation and the School of Business of the University of Wisconsin-Madison entitled "Productivity Measurement in Regulated Industries," held in Madison in 1979.

2. See Jorgenson and Griliches, 1967; Denison, 1969; Jorgenson and Griliches, 1972*a*; Denison, 1972; Jorgenson and Griliches, 1972*b*. The papers were gathered together under the title "The Measurement of Productivity" in the *Survey of Current Business,* May 1972, Part 2.

3. At a conference of the National Commission on Productivity. The full proceedings were published under the title *Conference on an Agenda for Economic Research on Productivity,* Washington, D.C.: U.S. Government Printing Office, 1973.

4. Total factor (or multifactor) productivity and labor productivity can be related to one another in the following way: Total factor productivity may be viewed as one of three factors into which labor productivity can be decomposed; the other two factors are tangible capital per worker-hour and labor quality per worker-hour (Fabricant, 1968).

5. It should be mentioned, however, that the greater rate of retardation of productivity growth abroad does not indicate that the gap between the United States and other countries, which had been narrowing prior to 1973, had become stabilized. In every case but two, the declines in the rate were from so high a relative level of productivity growth, compared with the United States, that even the bigger decline did not bring their rates down to ours. The productivity gap continued to narrow—another source of worry over the productivity situation in our country.

6. The BLS's analyses are summarized in Marks's presentation before the Joint Economic Committee in the hearings cited above (Marks, 1978). See also Denison, 1973.

7. See the National Bureau of Economic Research (NBER) study for the Council on Wage and Price Evaluation (Ruggles, 1977), and the discussion in the NBER study for the Bureau of the Census on the measurement of inventories (Foss, Fromm, and Rottenberg, forthcoming).

8. In this connection, see the discussion in the appendix to Zarnowitz and Moore (1977).

9. A study by Joel Popkin (1979) for the National Research Council panel marks a good beginning.

10. A major factor here is the rate of depreciation or obsolescence of knowledge, about which very little is known. Assumptions fill the gap, as in Kendrick's estimate mentioned below. An interesting effort to obtain objective information by using data on patent renewals suggests a much higher rate of obsolescence (on the kind of knowledge generally patented) than is commonly assumed (Pakes and Schankerman, 1978). A similar gap occurs in the data needed to estimate the contribution of growth in the tangible capital stock. The rates of depreciation and obsolescence on plant and equipment are based on

the somewhat arbitrary rates collected by the Internal Revenue Service and accepted by it for tax purposes. For a theoretically appealing effort to estimate tangible capital consumption more accurately, see the paper by R.S. Coen (1980).

11. The estimates he cited referred to real national income per person employed, and he compared the rate of change during 1969–1973 with that of 1973–1976. But these differences matter little as regards the essential picture traced from the figures given earlier.

12. See particularly the paper by Clark (1978) and the comments made by Norsworthy and Denison.

13. Under the joint auspices of the Bureau of the Budget and the Bureau of Labor Statistics (BLS, 1947).

REFERENCES

Bureau of Economic Analysis, 1973, *Long Term Economic Growth,* 1860–1970, Washington, D.C.: U.S. Department of Commerce, Part 5.

Bureau of Labor Statistics, 1947, *Summary of Proceedings of Conference on Productivity, October 28–29, 1946,* Bulletin No. 913, Washington, D.C.: U.S. Government Printing Office.

Christensen, L. R., D. Cummings, and D. W. Jorgensen, 1978, "Productivity Growth, 1947–73: An International Comparison," in *The Impact of International Trade and Investment on Employment,* edited by W.G. Dewald, Washington, D.C.: U.S. Government Printing Office.

Christensen, L. R., and D. W. Jorgenson, 1979, *U.S. Input, Output, Saving and Wealth,* Cambridge, Mass.: Harvard Institute of Economic Research.

Clark, Peter K., 1978, "Capital Formation and the Recent Productivity Slowdown," *Journal of Finance,* June.

Coen, R. S., 1980, "Alternative Measures of Capital and Its Rate of Return in U.S. Manufacturing," in Usher (1980).

Council of Economic Advisers, 1979, Annual Report, in *Economic Report of the President,* Washington D.C.: U.S. Government Printing Office.

Daly, Keith, and Arthur Neef, 1978, "Productivity and Unit Labor Costs in 11 Industrial Countries, 1977," *Monthly Labor Review,* November.

Denison, Edward F., 1978*a,* "The Drop in Productivity after 1973," Statement before the Joint Economic Committee, Special Study on Economic Change, June 8, Part 2, Washington, D.C.: U.S. Government Printing Office, pp. 490–93.

———, 1978*b,* "Effects of Selected Changes in the Institutional and Human Environment upon Output per Unit of Input," *Survey of Current Business,* January.

———, 1974, *Accounting for U.S. Economic Growth,* Washington, D.C.: Brookings.

———, 1973, "The Shift to Services and the Rate of Productivity Change," *Survey of Current Business,* October.

———, 1972, "Final Comments," *Survey of Current Business,* vol. 52, no. 5, May, Part 2, pp. 95–110.

_____, 1969, "Some Major Issues in Productivity Analysis: An Examination of Estimates by Jorgenson and Griliches," *Survey of Current Business,* vol. 49, no. 5, May, Part 2, pp. 1–27.

Fabricant, Solomon, 1979, *The Economic Growth of the United States: Perspective and Prospective,* Montreal: C.D. Howe Research Institute; Washington, D.C.: National Planning Association.

_____, 1978, "Productivity Growth: Purpose, Process, Prospects and Policy," Prepared for the National Center for Productivity and Quality of Working Life in the Joint Economic Committee, Special Study on Economic Change, June 8, Part 2, Washington, D.C.: U.S. Government Printing Office, pp. 501–31.

_____, 1974, "Perspective on Productivity Research," *Review of Income and Wealth,* September.

_____, 1968, "Productivity," in *International Encyclopedia of the Social Sciences,* edited by David L. Sills, New York: Macmillan and Free Press, pp. 523–36.

Foss, Murray, Gary Fromm, and Irving Rottenberg, forthcoming, *Measurement of Business Inventories,* Economic Research Report 3, Washington, D.C.: U.S. Department of Commerce, Bureau of the Census.

Griliches, Zvi, ed., 1971, *Price Indexes and Quality Change,* Cambridge, Mass.: Harvard University Press.

Jorgenson, D. W., and Z. Griliches, 1972*a,* "Issues in Growth Accounting: Final Reply," *Survey of Current Business,* vol. 52, no. 5, May, Part 2, p. 111.

_____, 1972*b,* "Issues in Growth Accounting: A Reply to Edward F. Denison," *Survey of Current Business,* vol. 52, no. 5, May, Part 2, pp. 65–94.

_____, 1967, "The Explanation of Productivity Change," *Review of Economic Studies,* vol. 34, no. 99, pp. 249–83.

Kendrick, J. W., 1979, Appendix 3, in *Reaching a Higher Standard of Living,* January, Office for Economic Research, New York Stock Exchange.

Kendrick, J. W., and Vaccara, B. N., eds., 1980, *New Developments in Productivity Measurement,* Chicago: University of Chicago Press.

Lancaster, Kelvin, 1977, "The Measurement of Changes in Quality," *Review of Income and Wealth,* June.

Marks, J. A., 1978, "Productivity Trends and Prospects," Statement before the Joint Economic Committee, Special Study on Economic Change, June 8, Part 2, Washington, D.C.: U.S. Government Printing Office, pp. 480–86.

Pakes, Ariel, and M. A. Schankerman, 1978, "The Rate of Obsolescence of Knowledge, Research Gestation Lags, and the Private Rate of Return on Research Resources," Discussion Paper Series No. 78–13, New York: New York University, Center for Applied Economics.

Panel to Review Productivity Statistics, 1979, *The Measurement and Interpretation of Productivity,* Committee on National Statistics, Assembly of Behavioral and Social Sciences, National Research Council, Washington, D.C.: National Academy of Sciences.

Popkin, Joel, 1979, "Comparison of Industry Output Measures in Manufacturing," in Panel to Review Productivity Statistics (1979), Appendix.

Ruggles, Richard, 1977, *The Wholesale Price Index: Review and Evaluation,* Washington, D.C.: Executive Office of the President, Council on Wage and Price Stability.

Stigler, George J., and James K. Kindahl, 1970, *The Behavior of Industrial Prices,* New York: National Bureau of Economic Research.

Usher, Dan, ed., 1980, *The Measurement of Capital,* Chicago: University of Chicago Press.

Zarnowitz, Victor, and G. H. Moore, 1977, "The Recession and Recovery of 1973–76," *Explorations in Economic Research,* Fall, Appendix.

3 BASIC FORCES IN PRODUCTIVITY GROWTH

C. Lowell Harriss

3.1. INTRODUCTION

Technological advance, capital formation, human freedom—these three factors embrace much of what has led to rising productivity through the centuries. Today's enormous differences in productivity result from a complex of intertwined causes. The elements of most basic importance—in the past, now, and for the future—cannot be separated with precision. Human beings who grow up in the same environment achieve strikingly large differences in lifetime output.

Try to imagine the levels of living over the world, within the boundaries of any political entity called a nation, or within the same community if everyone in about the same age group produced at least half as much as the best! Actual achievements do demonstrate how very much can be done—and distressingly large shortfalls. Why?

With concern to "doing something" to improve productivity, one can think of various contexts for attempting change: the national (or local) economy, the particular business firm, the individual. Each offers opportunities for valuable study and humanely useful action. Of course, the national economy, the individual, and all in between are interrelated. Human

39

beings do everything that is done, except as nature sends sun, wind, and rain. Motivation and inherent personal capacities lead to differences in what men and women accomplish. So do the tangible and intangible resources with which we can work. These, including the conditions affecting personal motivation, are subject to more or less direct and conscious influence.

Most of the positive changes that count are more nearly spontaneous, like the "invisible hand," than describable by such terms as *planning* or *control*. Yet mankind's long history indicates that "we" do have some scope for deliberate, purposive, and collective action to make improvements. Even greater scope, I fear, exists for erecting impediments. But I get ahead of my story.

3.2. CHALLENGES TO "POLICY"

Productivity advance can be thought of in a meaningful sense as enhancing the ability of human beings to do what they really desire. Is there a proper role for "policy?" When, as happened in early 1979, the president of the United States, his Council of Economic Advisers, and *all* members of the Joint Economic Committee agree that productivity is a matter of public (national) policy, Americans should take notice.

Individuals and families have and utilize, or fail to utilize, potentials for improving their own productivity. The potentials differ, but we all have *some*. Personal choices are largely personal. Proposals to force "us" to do better abound. The morality of one individual or group imposing something on others—perhaps under the guise of "being for their own good"—presents profound problems (at least for me). Yet coercive action exists all around.

Children cannot possibly know what they have not yet learned. They cannot judge the fruits, good or bad, from education, training, discipline, the cultivation of imagination, and so on. Adults, too, suffer from incompleteness of knowledge; thus, we have inadequate bases for judging what is in our own interest. Let us recognize potential conflicts of a truly disturbing nature in anything that involves the imposition—by a majority, a Congress, a civil service—of ideas or conditions. Taxes and regulations are examples of such coercion. The moral limits on the acceptability of compulsion, even through majority rule, are not determinable with any consensus. "Public policy" does exert influence. "Collective" actions *do* affect persons in varied walks of life. We may have had no part in some decisions influencing our productivity. We would often be utterly without competence to make choices that rest upon informed comparison of alternatives. Even now, for example, a majority of Americans would probably approve the tax on corporate income, a tax that in fact diminishes their own welfare.

Our leaders are probably right in concluding that productivity has enough importance for enough people to justify placing it on the list of proper concerns of collective (governmental) action. In reality, national defense, policing, and some other concerns that we have long treated as governmental do affect productivity. To some extent, the actual results are positive; to some extent, negative.

What are the realistic prospects of doing more good than harm through any changes in governmental policy? Risks of net disadvantage are not small. In actual life, how do politically made choices get formed? How do bureaucracies and the military operate as compared with the marketplace and the nonprofit sector (such as nongovernmental universities)? One should be skeptical of assertions that more governmental action will in fact improve human performance.

Let us look at three broad subjects affecting productivity: capital formation, technological progress, and freedom against regulation.

3.3. CAPITAL FORMATION

Capital formation in the United States in recent years has not been high enough to meet what I believe are the general expectations of most Americans. Fuzziness in definition does invite argumentation about unsatisfactory lack of precision regarding "adequacy of capital formation." Some economists deride the conclusion that Americans will not have enough capital. Yet I believe that certain points clearly deserve attention.

Whether or not we face a "capital shortage" may be a matter of definition. Markets *will* balance the quantities supplied with those demanded—at some price. Today, corporate-earning and interest-rate yields seem to me low after allowing for inflation. Real yields are low not because—by historical standards or in comparison with other lands—*net new* savings are pouring great supplies of funds into the market. Weaknesses on the demand side must account for some of the situation.

Business demand has hardly corresponded with the growth of the labor force. If it had, we would have seen that the net real savings available to business have remained below the levels required to finance the improvement in living standards that we seem to desire. The money-creating mechanism will not do the job.

Capital to improve the environment (air and water pollution) and perhaps the conditions of job safety and health have required large amounts for results that do not get into the measurements of output. Government use of savings also includes the financing of projects whose products are difficult to measure. Housing takes large amounts of saving; inflation has confirmed the wisdom of past decisions to commit families to debt for housing. The productivity of capital in housing can hardly be compared with the fruits of equal investment in industry. Casual observation would indicate that over a significantly wide margin, productivity in business expansion and modernization would be appreciably higher than in housing—we speak, to repeat, of some billions at the margin, not the total amounts. In America today, however, the building of housing and its myriad elements have strong partisans. Questioning the use of capital in such ways may arouse quite considerable opposition.

The gross benefits from capital accumulation are enormous. But there is a cost—the sacrifice of benefits from consumption now. One might suggest that ideally each person should decide for himself or herself about the rate of capital formation from the income available. Markets, however, work less well than we should like in relating personal benefits to personal costs. Benefits flow to human beings in their capacities as employees working with capital supplied by others. Benefits flow to human beings as consumers receiving goods and services made possible by the capital provided by others. These two types of benefits are not matched fully by rewards to the suppliers of capital. Or so it seems to me.

Externalities and elements somewhat like "consumers surplus" flow from capital, but not in forms that enhance the incentives and the ability of savers to enlarge the flow of new capital. The monetary rewards from saving (interest, dividends, rents, and net capital gains), plus the benefits in the form of personal (family) security from the ownership of property, will not, I submit, give signals adequate for measuring the full fruits to all who will benefit directly and indirectly from additions of capital.

In the United States the outlook for new saving and capital formation has been a matter of concern for a decade or so. Bottlenecks during the boom of 1973 showed that production capacity was smaller than had been assumed. The New York Stock Exchange sponsored a study looking into the 1980s and predicted a shortfall of considerable magnitude. Other inquiries during the 1970s used a variety of methods and assumptions and reached varying conclusions. One of the most widely respected was made by the U.S. Department of Commerce staff; it concluded that for the near future the more or less generally accepted goals could not be met without an increase of approximately one-tenth in investment in industry—more than one percentage point of gross national product. Since then, the figures for energy needs have risen markedly, and increasing doubt has been raised about the productivity of large capital outlays for environmental purposes. Net savings rates have sagged—along with the net capital growth potential. The savings decline as a percentage of income may be only a temporary phenomenon. If it is more lasting, the growth of productivity will suffer. Some of the authors who have addressed these issues include Malkiel (1979), Clark (1978), and Lindsay (1979).

Is there then a "proper" role for collective action to modify the economic framework to encourage saving? Would it be "right" for Congress to bias or to tilt taxation—and government's own spending policies—to induce more capital formation than today or more than would occur under as nearly neutral a policy as possible? The issues are not simple. Perhaps there *is* a role for mature wisdom to serve the young, the weak, and the ignorant in what large portions of such groups would see as their own interest if they were fully informed and competent. Would such a policy deserve support—if one is possible?

Politics being what we observe at times, one might well settle for reducing—eliminating if possible—those anticapital biases of the present system.

One possible source of savings would be federal budget surpluses. Even a reduction in deficits (which have been large relative to net savings) would reduce the federal government's use of savings that could go for financing the production of real capital. The prospects of budget surpluses seem remote. Curbing the growth of spending is difficult, and pressures for tax relief are strong.

Much congressional support exists for proposals to give tax relief for savings or for some of the interest and dividend income as a stimulus to private saving. The effectivenesss of such proposals seems questionable—not as a form of tax relief but as encouraging net increases in saving.

3.4. TECHNOLOGICAL PROGRESS

Scientific and technological advances (broadly conceived) have brought incalculable advantages in productivity. Many are striking and obvious, many indirect. Often, accident has played a part. The potentials, no less than the past achievements, must be so great that deliberate encouragement of the advance of knowledge should be high on a priority list of the "public business." Money and skill devoted to the pursuits of science have multiplied mankind's power to satisfy desires.

The "general" desirability of encouraging research and development will be clear. But being confident of something "in general" does not suffice to define the "in particulars." And action must always be specific. What projects can best be done? Resources of talent and funds are always limited, and any research effort is at a cost. The business firm has its own considerations about allocating funds and staff to research. Next year's "bottom line," we now hear, weighs too heavily in many firms. Academic institutions and governmental agencies have their limits. Where effort goes into the unknown, risks of disappointment are great, failures are frequent, and payoffs may be distant.

My personal instincts have long tended to support great freedom for research and large appropriations where collective funds are involved. Positive externalities can be·huge. Though I am generally skeptical of the desirability of a large, or larger, political sector and higher taxes, more governmental support for the advance of knowledge would probably be amply justified. The practical problems are difficult. Bases for the inexcusable waste justifying "golden fleece" awards are to be expected; examples of apparently foolish projects will appear. The parties directly involved will be biased, to some extent by personal interests and also, I expect, by greater familiarity with their own subjects than with others'. The management of publicly financed research presents many problems. Some are tied to national defense and security. The use of findings from publicly financed research for private benefit (patents on governmentally financed projects) will raise problems. And so on.

The current concern about productivity should spur thinking about how best to deploy governmental resources for research. My own competence does not provide qualification to contribute more to the discussion than the general admonition: Err on the side of expansion, imagination, and freedom.

A distressing decline in the rate of productivity increase in the United States in recent years accentuates concern about research and development (R&D). Total efforts have not risen as might have been expected from earlier trends. After adjusting for inflation, total spending by government, industry, universities, and other agencies at the end of the 1970s was not much different from that at the beginning. Questions are raised about the allocation of resources for research, especially the large amounts done for government. Was too much directed to space programs? How wise is the allocation in defense efforts? Medical efforts? Will the vast outlays for synthetic fuels and other energy needs divert skilled human talent and equipment from alternatives with high potential?

Businesses have shifted more of their effort to aspects of development and applications with near-term benefits at the expense of more basic and fundamental projects. Inflation with high nominal interest rates discourages sacrifices now for a future many years distant; outlays whose fruits are expected within a few years become relatively more attractive. But the advances that greatly increase productivity often require fundamental basic research that takes many years.

Estimates of the benefits from past successes show some exceedingly high returns. One group of experts made detailed studies of seventeen specific innovations (Mansfield et al., 1977, Chapter 10). None was a major breakthrough. The investigation included benefits beyond those that the company itself realized—that is, estimates of gains outside the market's calculations, or "social gains." The median total return—for society as a whole, including, but not limited to, the company—was around 56 percent a year. Clearly, the total benefits were enormous relative to the costs. Various other studies have also found returns greatly exceeding 30 percent. Yet in many cases the benefits are much smaller, especially those obtained by the businesses making the effort. Of the seventeen innovations referred to above, the benefit for the company was less than 10 percent a year for six. Risks of failure obviously differ widely.

3.5. FREEDOM

Results depend upon human actions, an observation that seems trite and obvious but one whose significance is sometimes slighted. Crucial to what we accomplish must be our freedom from limiting restraints.[1] Liberty should be thought of as a "resource" for productivity.

The concepts of freedom and liberty may appear somewhat out of fashion. More accurately, not only were restraints in fashion in Galileo's day, they are often in fashion. A person who would now invoke the idea of laissez-faire as a positive element for progress may inspire skeptical, even antagonistic, responses. Yet I submit that deliberate attention to freedom as a *means* (as well as an *end* in itself) can help to improve performance. Today, more so than five years ago, with awareness of the burdens of taxation, restriction, red tape, and regulation upon regulation, such concern quite properly gains force.

One aspect of freedom involves the extent of restriction by and from others. We think especially of nonmarket forces, chiefly through some use of the compulsion of government—more avoidable than inevitable. The increases in coercion have come from many sides and for many reasons. Several find powerful support in persuasive arguments. Each regulation or set of restraints should be examined on its own. To support or to condemn rule *A* or routine *B* as part of a blanket generalization can be more dangerous than helpful; moreover, such a stance does not conform to professional standards of responsibility. Yet the *total* in itself may have significance beyond anything understandable from knowledge of one or a few cases. A business firm, for example, faces a total of regulations, few of which are known to the national, state, and local lawmakers or a bureaucracy setting up one or two. What may seem good, in itself innocuous as it adds nothing appreciable as a restriction, becomes part of a mass that adds greatly to burdens on productivity. Union rules can also work in the same direction.

The results in the form of "drags" on creativity, energy, imagination, and initiative can never be measured. Who can know what might have developed if governmental and private restraints on freedom had been much fewer? We do now have some estimates of the dollar costs of regulation, and the figures command attention. Yet burdens of a profoundly serious nature can never be included fully in the measure.

Genius is rare. The combination of circumstances that have—or could have—produced truly great breakthroughs occur only rarely. Yet there have been some. And there are many more examples of less striking, but nonetheless highly valuable, cases. Mercantilism and its modern counterparts hamper human initiatives. Regulation can stifle, retard, hold back. Experience seems to me to teach a lesson not to be forgotten. One aspect of human nature will lead some men and women, if they are able to do so, to use the restrictive powers of government or some other force in ways that will hamper others. The conditions for innovation will suffer. Local codes for building construction, labor featherbedding, and occupational licensing are forms of restraints that slow productivity. And taxes as "human creations" now through much of the world impose impediments whose seriousness we probably underestimate.

The broadening of the market, the expansion of trading areas, will bring benefits of various kinds. The challenges of competition stimulate productivity growth. Barriers to trade retard improvement.[2]

Freedom is sometimes thought of as opportunity, as distinguished from the absence of restraint. Education, health, and other factors play a role in enlarging practical ability. Without entering a discussion of terminology and definition, I return to capital, broadly conceived, as an element that influences productivity. Here is a dimension of the expansion of opportunity. Much of what we designate as improved productivity results from the addition of capital—funds used to pay for physical productive facilities (including inventory) and for the financing of transactions (including payment of wages).

The *enlargement* of freedom in the form of opportunity relies to varying degrees and in many ways on capital accumulation. The addition of capital results from an excess of income over consumption. The difference between what is produced and what is consumed constitutes the source for adding to productive capacity. The ability and willingness to save—to go without something obtainable now to get advantages in the future—must make a crucial difference in the nature of the future. To what extent are people "future-oriented?" Are they willing to save? Are they able to do so?

Another aspect of opportunity involves personal incentives. Income (rewards) related to accomplishment can influence results. Profit sharing must offer unexploited potentials. Very high personal income tax rates are receiving increasing attention as adversely affecting incentives for more and more persons. Although anything like precision in measurement and estimation will be impossible, there must be a strong presumption that beyond some point, differing from person to person and situation to situation, "working for government" has rather less appeal than does leisure.

The effects of different amounts of freedom on productivity can hardly be measured. So many factors contribute to the total of accomplishments over decades. Human beings and cultures differ. For many of us, certainly, restrictions will hamper achievements—and freedom will make more possible.

The breaking down of feudal restrictions, the lowering of international trade barriers, and other liberalizing forces of the nineteenth century in parts of Europe can be cited as helping to explain progress then. But many forces were operating, including technological advance that in itself benefited from freedom. More recently, the contrast between regimented economies—in communist and other totalitarian areas—and economies with greater freedom, such as in West Germany, France, and Japan, can be cited. Yet figures must be used with caution.[3] The moves of dictatorial governments to alter the planning system by employing more freedom illustrate the general conclusions. Other evidence appears persuasively in a recent volume (Wanniski, 1978).

3.6. CONCLUDING COMMENT

Whether or not collective action through government—net, on balance, after considering *all* aspects—can really do much to enable human beings to improve productivity is a topic calling for continuing attention. Given the realities of politics, one must restrain any expression of optimism. Perhaps "sunset laws," which require the periodic reexamination of established regulations, do have promise as a means of getting rid of obsolete intervention. I am not sure. Reduction of high marginal tax rates would seem to me possible. The "philosopher-king" ideal tempts us to seek new methods through politics. Possibilities of good exist, but action should rest on full analysis of realities.

NOTES

1. Japan presents an example that may conflict with my generalizations. We should try to learn from its amazing record.
2. For some specific group, it can be argued, the "infant-industry" possibility may have merit. Moving forward on the learning curve can at times do wonders in cost reduction.
3. For evidence and discussion of figures, see Bergson (1978).

REFERENCES

Bergson, Abram, 1978, *Productivity and the Social System: The USSR and the West,* Cambridge, Mass.: Harvard University Press.

Clark, Peter K., 1978, "Capital Formation and the Recent Productivity Slow-down," *Journal of Finance,* June.

Lindsay, Robert, ed., 1979, *The Nation's Capital Needs: Three Studies* (by Daniel M. Holland and Stewart D. Myers, Joshua Rowen and George H. Sorter, and Robert Lindsay), New York: Committee for Economic Development.

Malkiel, Barton G., 1979, "The Capital Formation Problem in the United States," *Journal of Finance,* vol. 34, no. 2, May, pp. 291–306.

Mansfield, Edwin, et al., 1977, *The Production and Application of New Industrial Technology,* New York: W.W. Norton.

Wanniski, Jude, 1978, *The Way the World Works: How Economies Fail—and Succeed,* New York: Basic Books.

4 CAPITAL FORMATION AND U.S. PRODUCTIVITY GROWTH, 1948-1976

Barbara M. Fraumeni and Dale W. Jorgenson

4.1. INTRODUCTION

Rapid growth of the U.S. economy during the postwar period has been sustained by the highest rate of capital formation in U.S. economic history. The postwar performance of the U.S. economy is all the more remarkable in view of the experience of the 1930s, when growth was negligible and the rate of capital formation was severely depressed. Capital formation in the form of tangible assets dropped precipitously after the cyclical peak in economic activity in 1973, and economic growth has slowed measurably. The revival of capital formation is clearly the key to reestablishment of postwar trends in economic growth in the United States.

   The purpose of this study is to analyze the interrelationship between capital formation and economic growth in the United States over the period 1948-1976.[1] We begin with a brief overview of the historical record. The growth of the U.S. economy from 1948 to 1976, as measured by the average rate of growth of gross private domestic product, was 3.44 percent per year. By contrast, Christensen and Jorgenson (1970, 1973) have shown that the average annual rate of growth of gross private domestic product from 1929 to 1939 was slightly negative. Kuznets (1961) has estimated that the growth

49

rate of gross national product from 1869 to 1948 averaged 4.23 percent per year.

To assess the role of capital formation in the growth of the U.S. economy from 1948 to 1976, we compare the contribution of capital with the contributions of other productive inputs and the rate of technical change, defined as the rate of growth of output, holding all inputs fixed. The rate of technical change includes changes in technology at the sectoral level and the impact of reallocations of value added, capital input, and labor input among sectors. We combine the results for forty-six industrial sectors to analyze the contribution of capital to the growth of the output of the private domestic sector of the U.S. economy. The contribution of capital input exceeds that of the rate of technical change for sixteen of the twenty-eight years included in our study. For the period as a whole, the average contribution of capital input exceeds that of the rate of technical change.

Our analysis of the role of capital in the growth of the U.S. economy over the period 1948–1976 is based on an aggregate production account in current and constant prices, constructed on the basis of principles outlined by Jorgenson (1980). The fundamental accounting identity for the aggregate production account is that value added is equal to the sum of property and labor compensation for the private domestic sector of the U.S. economy. Our aggregate production account includes data on aggregate value added and aggregate capital and labor input in current and constant prices. Finally, it includes the rate of aggregate technical change.

Fraumeni and Jorgenson (1980) present sectoral production accounts for the forty-six industrial sectors. These accounts include data on sectoral output and sectoral intermediate, capital, and labor input in current and constant prices, together with the rate of sectoral technical change. By combining data from our aggregate production account and from our sectoral production accounts, we can express the rate of aggregate technical change as a weighted sum of rates of sectoral technical change and terms corresponding to the effects of the redistribution of value added, capital input, and labor input among sectors.

4.2. SECTORAL VALUE ADDED

Following Jorgenson (1980), we employ sectoral value-added functions in constructing an aggregate production account. Sectoral value added is expressed as a function of sectoral capital and labor inputs and time. We combine the sectoral value-added functions with necessary conditions for producer equilibrium in each sector. These conditions imply that the elasticities of the quantity of sector value added with respect to the quantities of sectoral capital and labor inputs are equal to the shares of these inputs in sectoral value added.

Sectoral value added is defined as the sum of the values of sectoral capital input and sectoral labor input:

$$p_V^i V_i = p_K^i K_i + p_L^i L_i, \tag{4.1}$$

where p_V^i, p_K^i, and p_L^i are prices of sectoral value added, capital input, and labor input, and V_i, K_i, and L_i are the corresponding quantities. Using the definition of value added and the accounting identity between the value of sectoral output and the sum of the values of sectoral intermediate, capital, and labor inputs, we can express sectoral value added as the difference between the value of sectoral output and the value of sectoral intermediate input:

$$p_V^i V_i = p_i Z_i - p_X^i X_i,$$

where p_i and p_X^i are prices of sectoral output and intermediate input, and Z_i and X_i are the corresponding quantities.

To separate price and quantity components of sectoral value added, we represent sectoral output as a function of the quantity of sectoral value added and intermediate input, following Jorgenson (1980). Sectoral output is not represented as a function of time, so that changes in technology can be attributed to changes in the sectoral value-added functions. We combine the sectoral production functions with necessary conditions for producer equilibrium in each sector. These conditions imply that the elasticities of sectoral output with respect to the quantities of sectoral intermediate input and value added are equal to the shares of the value of intermediate input and value added in the value of sectoral output. We assume that the quantity of sectoral output is a translog function of the quantities of sectoral value added and intermediate input.

Considering data on sectoral output and intermediate input at any two discrete points of time, we can express the difference between successive logarithms of sectoral output as a weighted average of the difference between successive logarithms of sectoral intermediate input and value added with weights given by the average shares of sectoral intermediate input and value added in the value of sectoral output:

$$\ell n\, Z_{i,t} - \ell n\, Z_{i,t-1} = \bar{v}_X^i \left(\ell n\, X_{i,t} - \ell n\, X_{i,t-1} \right)$$
$$+ \bar{v}_V^i \left(\ell n\, V_{i,t} - \ell n\, V_{i,t-1} \right), \tag{4.2}$$

where

$$\bar{v}_X^i = (\tfrac{1}{2})(v_{X,t}^i + v_{X,t-1}^i);$$
$$\bar{v}_V^i = (\tfrac{1}{2})(v_{V,t}^i + v_{V,t-1}^i);$$

and

$$v_X^i = (p_X^i V_i)/(p_i Z_i);$$
$$v_V^i = (p_V^i X_i)/(p_i Z_i).$$

The difference between successive logarithms of sectoral value added can be expressed in terms of differences between successive logarithms of sectoral output and intermediate input and average value shares of sectoral intermediate input and value added:

$$\ell n \, V_{i,t} - \ell n \, V_{i,t-1} = \frac{1}{\bar{v}_V^i} \, (\ell n \, Z_{i,t} - \ell n \, Z_{i,t-1}) - \frac{\bar{v}_X^i}{\bar{v}_V^i} \, (\ell n \, X_t^i - \ell n \, X_{t-1}^i).$$

Following Jorgenson (1980), we refer to this expression for the quantity of sectoral value added as the *translog index of sectoral value added*. The corresponding index of the price of sectoral value added is equal to the ratio of sectoral value added to the translog quantity index.

4.3. AGGREGATE PRODUCTION

Our multisectoral model of production and technical change includes value-added functions for forty-six industrial sectors of the U.S. economy. The model also includes market equilibrium conditions:

$$K_k = \Sigma K_{ki},$$
$$L_\ell = \Sigma L_{\ell i}. \tag{4.3}$$

Each type of aggregate capital input K_k is the sum of the corresponding sectoral capital inputs, K_{ki}, where the subscript k ranges over the four legal forms of organization and the six types of assets described by Fraumeni and Jorgenson (1980). Similarly, each type of aggregate capital input, L_ℓ, is the sum of the corresponding sectoral labor inputs, $L_{\ell i}$, where the subscript ℓ ranges over the different types of labor input described by Gollop and Jorgenson (1980).

We can define the prices of aggregate capital inputs, p_{Kk}, in terms of prices paid for each type of capital input in all forty-six sectors:

$$p_{Kk}K_k = p_{Kk}\Sigma K_{ki}$$
$$= \Sigma p_{Kk}^i K_{ki}. \tag{4.4}$$

The value of each type of aggregate capital input is equal to the sum of values over all sectors. The price of each type of aggregate capital input is equal to the ratio of the sum of values over all sectors to the sum of quantities over all sectors. Similarly, we can define the prices of aggregate labor inputs, $p_{L\ell}$, in terms of prices paid for each type of labor input in all forty-six sectors $p_{L\ell}^i$:

$$p_{L\ell}L_\ell = p_{L\ell}\Sigma L_{\ell i}$$
$$= \Sigma p_{L\ell}^i L_{\ell i}. \tag{4.5}$$

These prices of each type of aggregate labor input are equal to the ratio of the sum of values over all sectors to the sum of quantities over all sectors.

Finally, we can define aggregate value added as the sum of value added in all sectors:

$$p_V V = \Sigma p_V^i V_i, \tag{4.6}$$

where p_V is the price and V is the quantity of aggregate value added. The quantity of aggregate value added is the sum of the corresponding sectoral quantities of value added:

$$V = \Sigma V_i. \tag{4.7}$$

Our aggregate model of production and technical change is based on an aggregate production function, representing the quantity of aggregate value added as a function of the quantities of aggregate capital and labor input and time. We combine the aggregate production function with necessary conditions for producer equilibrium at the aggregate level. These conditions imply that the elasticities of aggregate output with respect to the quantities of aggregate capital and labor input are equal to the shares of the value of these inputs in aggregate value added. We assume that the quantity of aggregate output is a translog function of aggregate capital and labor input.

Considering data on aggregate value added and aggregate capital and labor inputs at any two discrete points of time, we can express the average rate of aggregate technical change as the difference between successive logarithms of aggregate output and a weighted average of differences between

successive logarithms of aggregate capital and labor input with weights
given by average value shares in the two periods:

$$\bar{v}_t = \ln V_t - \ln V_{t-1} - \bar{v}_K(\ln K_t - \ln K_{t-1})$$
$$- \bar{v}_L (\ln L_t - \ln L_{t-1}), \tag{4.8}$$

where

$$\bar{v}_K = (\tfrac{1}{2})(v_{K,t} + v_{K,t-1});$$
$$\bar{v}_L = (\tfrac{1}{2})(v_{L,t} + v_{L,t-1});$$
$$\bar{v}_t = (\tfrac{1}{2})(v_{t,t} + v_{t,t-1});$$

and

$$v_K = (p_K K)/(p_V V);$$
$$v_L = (p_L L)/(p_V V).$$

Following Jorgenson (1980), we refer to this expression for the average rate
of aggregate technical change as the *translog index of aggregate technical
change*.

Similarly, we represent the quantities of aggregate capital and labor input as functions of the quantities of their components. We combine the aggregate input functions with necessary conditions for producer equilibrium
at the aggregate level. These conditions imply that the elasticities of aggregate capital and labor input with respect to the quantities of their components are equal to the shares of the value of these components in the value
of the corresponding aggregate input. We assume that the quantities of aggregate capital and labor input are translog functions of their components.

Considering data on aggregate capital and labor inputs at any two discrete points of time, we can express the differences between successive logarithms of these inputs as weighted averages of differences between successive logarithms of their components with weights given by average value
shares in the two periods:

$$\ln K_t - \ln K_{t-1} = \Sigma \bar{v}_{Kk} (\ln K_{k,t} - \ln K_{k,t-1}),$$
$$\ln L_t - \ln L_{t-1} = \Sigma \bar{v}_{L\ell} (\ln L_{\ell,t} - \ln L_{\ell,t-1}), \tag{4.9}$$

where

$$\bar{v}_{Kk} = (\tfrac{1}{2})(v_{Kk,t} + v_{Kk,t-1});$$
$$\bar{v}_{L\ell} = (\tfrac{1}{2})(v_{L\ell,t} + v_{L\ell,t-1});$$

and

$$v_{Kk} = (p_{Kk}\, K_k)/\Sigma p_{Kk}\, K_k);$$
$$v_{L\ell} = (p_{L\ell}\, L_\ell)/\Sigma p_{L\ell}\, L_\ell).$$

Following Jorgenson (1980), we refer to these indexes as *translog indexes of aggregate capital and labor inputs,* respectively.

We take the values of aggregate capital and labor input to be equal to the sum of the values of their components:

$$p_K\, K = \Sigma p_{Kk}\, K_k,$$
$$p_L\, L = \Sigma p_{L\ell}\, L_\ell. \tag{4.10}$$

The prices of aggregate capital and labor inputs are equal to the ratios of the sum of values over all types of aggregate capital and labor inputs to the corresponding translog quantity indexes.

Combining the translog indexes of aggregate capital and labor inputs with the translog index of aggregate technical change, we can express the rate of aggregate technical change in the form:

$$\bar{v}_t = \ell n\, V_t - \ell n\, V_{t-1} - \bar{v}_K \cdot \Sigma \bar{v}_{Kk}\,(\ell n\, K_{k,t} - \ell n\, K_{k,t-1})$$
$$- \bar{v}_L \cdot \Sigma \bar{v}_{L\ell}\,(\ell n\, L_{\ell,t} - \ell n\, L_{\ell,t-1}). \tag{4.11}$$

4.4. GROWTH IN OUTPUT AND INPUTS

We first construct an aggregate production account for the private domestic sector of the U.S. economy. In Table 4.1, we give data on the prices and quantities of aggregate value added, capital input, and labor input. We present annual data for rates of growth of aggregate value added, capital input, and labor input and for the rate of aggregate technical change in Table 4.2. Value added grows rapidly throughout the period 1948-1973, with declines in 1949, 1954, 1958, and 1970 followed by sharp recoveries in 1950, 1955, 1959, and 1971-72.

The development of aggregate value added during the period 1973-1976 stands apart from earlier postwar experience. First, the magnitude of the decline in 1974 is without precedent during the period 1948-1973. Declines in 1949, 1954, 1958, and 1970 lasted for a single year and were less than 1 percent in magnitude. The decline in 1974 totaled 3.36 percent and continued into 1975 with a further drop of 0.42 percent. Taken together, these two years represent the most severe downturn of the U.S. economy since the

Table 4.1. Aggregate Input (Constant Prices of 1972), 1948-1976

Year	Value Added		Capital Input		Labor Input	
	Price	Quantity	Price	Quantity	Price	Quantity
1948	0.567	433.460	0.538	168.725	0.331	468.078
1949	0.559	431.110	0.515	179.214	0.331	448.406
1950	0.573	473.440	0.583	186.333	0.351	464.477
1951	0.613	506.596	0.583	199.194	0.400	486.236
1952	0.629	519.333	0.603	210.094	0.402	496.286
1953	0.626	544.783	0.592	217.375	0.419	507.090
1954	0.643	543.214	0.612	225.701	0.432	489.307
1955	0.647	583.907	0.655	232.550	0.446	504.689
1956	0.658	603.884	0.634	244.755	0.471	513.323
1957	0.669	617.530	0.623	254.391	0.498	511.784
1958	0.689	615.540	0.641	262.839	0.519	493.368
1959	0.690	658.980	0.691	267.194	0.528	511.672
1960	0.711	671.549	0.706	276.155	0.536	527.260
1961	0.714	688.859	0.704	284.434	0.564	516.297
1962	0.726	725.385	0.738	290.781	0.583	535.047
1963	0.726	760.729	0.753	300.720	0.604	539.000
1964	0.738	801.465	0.788	312.669	0.625	551.639
1965	0.761	847.455	0.843	327.338	0.648	569.814
1966	0.788	897.541	0.863	346.095	0.687	594.149
1967	0.806	918.834	0.847	367.150	0.714	601.364
1968	0.834	960.071	0.863	384.033	0.765	613.160
1969	0.885	989.125	0.900	402.805	0.816	628.092
1970	0.908	988.608	0.846	422.055	0.866	624.632
1971	0.949	1022.059	0.906	435.294	0.933	616.898
1972	1.000	1082.066	1.000	450.742	1.000	631.324
1973	1.088	1125.855	1.050	471.870	1.109	657.840
1974	1.183	1088.709	1.020	496.083	1.184	660.205
1975	1.277	1084.151	1.126	511.289	1.255	644.242
1976	1.353	1156.370	1.277	518.239	1.348	669.452

1930s. The recovery of aggregate value added, beginning with growth of 6.45 percent in 1976, is in line with earlier postwar recoveries, suggesting a permanent loss in growth from the downturn that lasted from 1973 to 1975.

Turning to the growth of capital input, we find that declines in value added during the period 1948-1976 were followed by reductions in the rate of growth of capital input one period later. This pattern continued into the period 1973-1976. The growth rate of capital input reached a peak at 5 per-

Table 4.2. Growth in Aggregate Input and the Aggregate Rate of Technical Change, 1949-1976

Year	Value Added	Capital Input	Labor Input	Rate of Technical Change
1948-1949	-0.0054	0.0603	-0.0429	-0.0014
1949-1950	0.0937	0.0390	0.0352	0.0570
1950-1951	0.0677	0.0667	0.0458	0.0138
1951-1952	0.0248	0.0533	0.0205	-0.0081
1952-1953	0.0478	0.0341	0.0215	0.0215
1953-1954	-0.0029	0.0376	-0.0357	0.0045
1954-1955	0.0722	0.0299	0.0310	0.0417
1955-1956	0.0336	0.0512	0.0170	0.0031
1956-1957	0.0223	0.0386	-0.0030	0.0092
1957-1958	-0.0032	0.0327	-0.0366	0.0064
1958-1959	0.0682	0.0164	0.0364	0.0398
1959-1960	0.0189	0.0330	0.0300	-0.0123
1960-1961	0.0254	0.0295	-0.0210	0.0259
1961-1962	0.0517	0.0221	0.0357	0.0215
1962-1963	0.0476	0.0336	0.0074	0.0295
1963-1964	0.0522	0.0390	0.0232	0.0225
1964-1965	0.0558	0.0458	0.0324	0.0177
1965-1966	0.0574	0.0557	0.0418	0.0097
1966-1967	0.0234	0.0591	0.0121	-0.0084
1967-1968	0.0439	0.0450	0.0194	0.0138
1968-1969	0.0298	0.0477	0.0241	-0.0040
1969-1970	-0.0005	0.0467	-0.0055	-0.0162
1970-1971	0.0333	0.0309	-0.0125	0.0283
1971-1972	0.0571	0.0349	0.0231	0.0291
1972-1973	0.0397	0.0458	0.0411	-0.0034
1973-1974	-0.0336	0.0500	0.0036	-0.0557
1974-1975	-0.0042	0.0302	-0.0245	-0.0018
1975-1976	0.0645	0.0135	0.0384	0.0365

cent in 1974, followed by growth rates of 3.02 percent in 1975 and 1.35 percent in 1976. The rate of growth of capital input in 1976 was the smallest over any year during the postwar period; however, the decline in the growth rate of capital input that took place from 1974 to 1976 is not out of line with the declines in value added that took place from 1973 to 1975.

The growth rate of capital input was positive throughout the period from 1948 to 1976. By comparison with the growth of capital input, the growth of labor input is considerably more uneven. Substantial declines in labor input coincided with declines in value added in 1949, 1954, 1958, and 1970; however, declines in labor input also took place in 1957, 1961, and 1971. The pattern of coincidence between declines in value added and in labor input was broken during the period 1973–1976. During this period, labor input declined in 1975, lagging behind the drop in value added that took place in 1974. The decline in labor input that took place in 1975 was modest in relation to the decline in value added in 1974 and 1975 and was not large by comparison with earlier postwar drops.

Finally, considering the pattern of technical change over the postwar period, we find that high rates of technical change are associated with recoveries in the growth of value added in 1950, 1955, 1959, 1971–72, and 1976. In addition, rapid growth in the level of technology took place during the period 1960–1966, which was also characterized by unusually rapid growth of value added, capital input, and labor input. The rate of technical change for 1973 was a negative 0.34 percent in 1973 at the peak of value added, repeating a pattern that emerged at the previous peak in 1969, when the rate of technical change was a negative 0.40 percent. The magnitude of the decline in the level of technology in 1974 was unprecedented in postwar experience at 5.56 percent. The continuation of declines in the level of technology for three years—1973, 1974, 1975—was also a new development.

4.5. CONTRIBUTION TO ECONOMIC GROWTH

We can express the rate of growth of aggregate value added as a weighted average of rates of growth of aggregate capital and labor inputs plus the rate of technical change. Growth rates of capital and labor inputs are weighted by the corresponding shares of each input in aggregate value added. We define the contributions of capital and labor input to the growth of output as the weighted growth rates of these inputs. In Table 4.3, we present the rate of growth of aggregate value added, the average value share of capital input, the contributions of capital and labor input to the growth of output, and the rate of technical change. The average value share of labor input is equal to unity less the average value share of capital input.

The average value share of capital input is very stable over the period 1948–1976, ranging from 0.3763 for 1948 and 1949 to 0.4251 for 1965 and 1966. Accordingly, the cyclical pattern relating growth in value added to the contributions of capital and labor inputs is virtually identical to the pattern relating growth in value added to growth in capital and labor inputs that we have examined previously. Comparing the contributions of capital and labor inputs and the rate of technical change as sources of growth of value

Table 4.3.   Contribution to Growth in Aggregate Output, 1949-1976

Year	Aggregate Value Added	Average Value Share of Capital Input	Capital Input	Labor Input	Rate of Technical Change
1948-1949	-0.0054	0.3763	0.0227	-0.0268	-0.0014
1949-1950	0.0937	0.3914	0.0152	0.0214	0.0570
1950-1951	0.0677	0.3869	0.0258	0.0281	0.0138
1951-1952	0.0248	0.3811	0.0203	0.0127	-0.0081
1952-1953	0.0478	0.3828	0.0130	0.0133	0.0215
1953-1954	-0.0029	0.3864	0.0145	-0.0219	0.0045
1954-1955	0.0722	0.3995	0.0119	0.0186	0.0417
1955-1956	0.0336	0.3972	0.0203	0.0102	0.0031
1956-1957	0.0223	0.3873	0.0150	-0.0018	0.0092
1957-1958	-0.0032	0.3903	0.0128	-0.0223	0.0064
1958-1959	0.0682	0.4015	0.0066	0.0218	0.0398
1959-1960	0.0189	0.4072	0.0134	0.0178	-0.0123
1960-1961	0.0254	0.4077	0.0120	-0.0124	0.0259
1961-1962	0.0517	0.4075	0.0090	0.0211	0.0215
1962-1963	0.0476	0.4089	0.0137	0.0044	0.0295
1963-1964	0.0522	0.4133	0.0161	0.0136	0.0225
1964-1965	0.0558	0.4221	0.0194	0.0187	0.0177
1965-1966	0.0574	0.4251	0.0237	0.0240	0.0097
1966-1967	0.0234	0.4213	0.0249	0.0070	-0.0084
1967-1968	0.0439	0.4171	0.0188	0.0113	0.0138
1968-1969	0.0298	0.4141	0.0198	0.0141	-0.0040
1969-1970	-0.0005	0.4059	0.0189	-0.0033	-0.0162
1970-1971	0.0333	0.4021	0.0124	-0.0074	0.0283
1971-1972	0.0571	0.4116	0.0144	0.0136	0.0291
1972-1973	0.0397	0.4105	0.0188	0.0243	-0.0034
1973-1974	-0.0336	0.3987	0.0200	0.0022	-0.0557
1974-1975	-0.0042	0.4045	0.0122	-0.0146	-0.0018
1975-1976	0.0645	0.4196	0.0057	0.0223	0.0365

added, we find that the contribution of capital input is positive throughout the period from 1948 to 1976 and relatively steady. By contrast, the contribution of labor input and the rate of technical change are negative for eight and nine of the twenty-eight periods, respectively, and are relatively uneven.

The contribution of capital input provides the largest single contribution to the growth of output in thirteen of the twenty-eight periods from 1948 to

1976. The contribution of labor input provides the largest contribution in four of these periods. Finally, the rate of technical change provides the largest contribution in eleven periods. Comparing the contribution of capital input with that of labor input, we find that the contribution of capital input is greater in eighteen of the twenty-eight periods. The contribution of capital input is greater than the rate of technical change in seventeen of the twenty-eight periods. Finally, the contribution of labor input is greater than the rate of technical change in only eleven of the twenty-eight periods.

We conclude that the contribution of capital input is the most important source of growth in output, that the rate of technical change is the next most important source, and that the contribution of labor input is the least important. This conclusion suggests a useful perspective on the severe recession and partial recovery of the U.S. economy over the period 1973–1976. The steep decline in aggregate value added in 1974 was associated with the sharp reversal in growth in the level of technology that began in 1973, reached its nadir in 1974, and extended into 1975. This was followed by a collapse in the growth in capital input that prolonged the downturn and weakened the recovery. By contrast, the contribution of labor input followed a course from 1973 to 1976 that was little different from that of earlier postwar recessions. To examine the pattern of the contributions of capital input and the rate of technical change in more detail, we can decompose these sources of growth into their components.

4.6. DECOMPOSITION OF CAPITAL INPUT

First, we can decompose the growth of aggregate capital input into components associated with growth in aggregate capital stock and in the quality of capital stock. We can define the quality of capital stock as an index that transforms aggregate capital stock at the beginning of the period into aggregate capital input during the period:

$$K_t = Q_{K,t} \cdot A_{t-1}, \tag{4.12}$$

where K_t is aggregate capital input, $Q_{K,t}$ is the quality of capital stock, and A_{t-1} is aggregate capital stock at the beginning of the period. Using the fact that the rate of growth of aggregate capital input can be expressed as the sum of the rate of growth of aggregate capital stock and the rate of growth of aggregate capital quality, we can express the contribution of aggregate capital input to the growth of output in terms of weighted rates of growth of aggregate capital stock and aggregate capital quality:

$$\bar{v}_K \, (\ln K_t - \ln K_{t-1}) = \bar{v}_K \, (\ln Q_{K,t} - \ln Q_{K,t-1})$$
$$+ \bar{v}_K \, (\ln A_{t-1} - \ln A_{t-2}). \tag{4.13}$$

We define the contributions of capital stock and its quality as the weighted growth rates of these sources of growth in output.

We present the quantity of capital stock for the private domestic sector of the U.S. economy for the period from 1948 to 1976 in Table 4.4. We also present an index of the quality of aggregate capital stock. In order to analyze the growth of capital input, we also provide rates of growth of capital stock and its quality. Finally, we show the contributions of capital stock and its quality to the growth of value added. We find that the growth of

Table 4.4.   Aggregate Capital Quality and Aggregate Capital Stock, 1948-1976

	Capital Input			Growth in Capital Input		Contributions to Growth in Capital Input	
Year	Capital Quality	Capital Stock	Year	Capital Quality	Capital Stock	Capital Quality	Capital Stock
1948	0.714	1616.505	1948–1949	0.0252	0.0351	0.0095	0.0132
1949	0.732	1674.299	1949–1950	0.0170	0.0220	0.0066	0.0086
1950	0.745	1711.526	1950–1951	0.0282	0.0386	0.0109	0.0149
1951	0.766	1778.854	1951–1952	0.0210	0.0322	0.0080	0.0123
1952	0.782	1837.129	1952–1953	0.0117	0.0224	0.0045	0.0086
1953	0.791	1878.696	1953–1954	0.0143	0.0233	0.0055	0.0090
1954	0.803	1922.962	1954–1955	0.0099	0.0200	0.0039	0.0080
1955	0.811	1961.864	1955–1956	0.0186	0.0325	0.0074	0.0129
1956	0.826	2026.752	1956–1957	0.0116	0.0270	0.0045	0.0105
1957	0.836	2082.280	1957–1958	0.0113	0.0214	0.0044	0.0083
1958	0.845	2127.250	1958–1959	0.0034	0.0130	0.0014	0.0052
1959	0.848	2155.192	1959–1960	0.0094	0.0236	0.0038	0.0096
1960	0.856	2206.645	1960–1961	0.0087	0.0209	0.0035	0.0085
1961	0.863	2253.193	1961–1962	0.0051	0.0170	0.0021	0.0069
1962	0.868	2291.746	1962–1963	0.0097	0.0239	0.0040	0.0098
1963	0.876	2347.279	1963–1964	0.0124	0.0266	0.0051	0.0110
1964	0.887	2410.478	1964–1965	0.0169	0.0290	0.0071	0.0122
1965	0.902	2481.358	1965–1966	0.0197	0.0360	0.0084	0.0153
1966	0.920	2572.243	1966–1967	0.0211	0.0379	0.0089	0.0160
1967	0.940	2671.667	1967–1968	0.0148	0.0301	0.0062	0.0126
1968	0.954	2753.431	1968–1969	0.0157	0.0320	0.0065	0.0133
1969	0.969	2843.081	1969–1970	0.0148	0.0319	0.0060	0.0129
1970	0.983	2935.221	1970–1971	0.0085	0.0224	0.0034	0.0090
1971	0.992	3001.629	1971–1972	0.0081	0.0267	0.0034	0.0110
1972	1.000	3082.935	1972–1973	0.0114	0.0344	0.0047	0.0141
1973	1.011	3190.930	1973–1974	0.0113	0.0387	0.0045	0.0154
1974	1.023	3316.938	1974–1975	0.0064	0.0238	0.0026	0.0096
1975	1.029	3396.910	1975–1976	0.0036	0.0099	0.0015	0.0042
1976	1.033	3430.874					

capital quality is an important source of growth of capital input, but it is dominated by the growth of capital stock. Both components of capital input have positive rates of growth throughout the period from 1948 to 1976. By comparison with the contribution of labor input and the rate of technical change, the contributions of both capital stock and its quality are relatively smooth.

We have observed that the growth of capital input declined in 1950, 1955, 1959, and 1971, following the declines in value added in 1949, 1954, 1958, and 1970. We find that the slowdown in the growth of capital input is associated with declines in rates of growth of both capital stock and its quality. This pattern persists into the downturn in the growth of capital input that took place in 1975 and 1976. In both years, the growth rates of capital quality and capital stock declined sharply. The growth rate of capital stock reached its postwar minimum in 1976, while the growth rate of the quality of capital stock in 1976 fell to a lower level than in any year in the postwar period except 1959. Since the average share of capital input in value added is very stable, these patterns carry over directly to the contributions of capital stock and its quality to the growth of value added.

4.7. DECOMPOSITION OF TECHNICAL CHANGE

We have decomposed the contribution of capital input, the most important source of growth in value added, into components associated with the contributions of capital stock and its quality.

Following Jorgenson (1980), we can express the translog index of aggregate technical change in terms of translog indexes of sectoral technical change in all sectors and changes in the distribution of value added and primary factors of production among sectors:

$$
\begin{aligned}
\bar{v}_t = \Sigma \frac{\bar{w}_j}{\bar{v}_V^j} \cdot \bar{v}_t^j &+ (\ell n \ V_t - \ell n \ V_{t-1}) - \Sigma \bar{w}_j \ (\ell n \ V_{j,t} - \ell n \ V_{j,t-1}) \\
&+ \Sigma \bar{w}_j \cdot \frac{\bar{v}_K^j}{\bar{v}_V^j} \Sigma \bar{v}_{Kk}^j \ (\ell n \ K_{kj,t} - \ell n \ K_{kj,t-1}) \\
&- \bar{v}_K \cdot \Sigma \bar{v}_{Kk} \ (\ell n \ K_{k,t} - \ell n \ K_{k,t-1}) \\
&+ \Sigma \bar{w}_j \cdot \frac{\bar{v}_L^j}{\bar{v}_V^j} \Sigma \bar{v}_{L\ell}^j \ (\ell n \ L_{\ell j,t} - \ell n \ L_{\ell j,t-1}) \\
&- \bar{v}_L \cdot \Sigma \bar{v}_{L\ell} \ (\ell n \ L_{\ell,t} - \ell n \ L_{\ell,t-1}), \qquad (4.14)
\end{aligned}
$$

where

$$
\bar{v}_V^j = (\tfrac{1}{2}) \ (v_{V,t}^j + v_{V,t-1}^j);
$$
$$
\bar{w}_j = (\tfrac{1}{2}) \ (w_{j,t} + w_{j,t-1});
$$

and

$$v_V^j = p_V^j \, V_j / p_j \, Z_j;$$
$$w_j = p_V^j \, V_j / \Sigma p_V^j V_j.$$

The first term in the expression we have given above for the aggregate rate of technical change is a weighted sum of sectoral rates of technical change with weights given by the ratio of the value of output in each sector to value added in that sector. The sum of these weights exceeds unity, since technical change in each sector contributes to the growth of sectoral output. It also contributes to the growth of sectoral output in other sectors through deliveries to demand for intermediate goods in these sectors. The second, third, and fourth terms in the expression for the aggregate rate of technical change correspond to differences between rates of growth of aggregate value added, capital input, and labor input and weighted averages of value added, capital input, and labor input in all sectors. These terms represent the contribution of redistributions of value added, capital input, and labor input among sectors to the aggregate rate of technical change. If the prices of value added are the same for all sectors or the quantities of value added in all sectors grow at the same rate, the term associated with the reallocation of value added among sectors is equal to zero. Similarly, the terms associated with reallocation of capital and labor inputs are equal to zero if the prices of these inputs are the same for all sectors or if the quantities of these inputs in all sectors grow at the same rate.

We present data for all four components of the aggregate rate of technical change for the period 1948-1976 in Table 4.5. The sum of these four components is equal to the rate of aggregate technical change given in Table 4.2. The weighted sum of rates of sectoral technical change is by far the most important source of the rate of aggregate technical change over the period 1949-1976. The impact of the reallocation of value added among sectors is negative for twenty of the twenty-eight periods and exceeds the impact of the weighted sum of rates of sectoral technical change in only six of the twenty-eight periods. The impact of reallocation of capital input on the rate of aggregate technical change is very small in every period and is negative for only four of the twenty-eight periods. The impact of the reallocation of labor input is small but not negligible and is negative for ten of the twenty-eight periods.

The period 1973-1976 stands out from the rest of the postwar period in a number of important respects. First, the decline in the aggregate level of technology in 1973 reflects the impact of a weighted sum of sectoral rates of technical change that was smaller than in any previous postwar period, par-

Table 4.5. Contribution to Growth in Aggregate Input and the Aggregate Rate of Technical Change, 1949-1976

Year	Sectoral Rates of Technical Change	Reallocation of:		
		Value Added	Capital Input	Labor Input
1948-1949	0.0144	-0.0174	0.0041	-0.0025
1949-1950	0.0606	-0.0080	0.0020	0.0024
1950-1951	0.0035	0.0064	0.0022	0.0016
1951-1952	-0.0008	-0.0086	0.0024	-0.0012
1952-1953	0.0316	-0.0102	0.0005	-0.0004
1953-1954	0.0076	-0.0009	0.0003	-0.0025
1954-1955	0.0522	-0.0117	0.0006	0.0006
1955-1956	0.0024	-0.0015	0.0011	0.0011
1956-1957	0.0087	0.0019	0.0012	-0.0025
1957-1958	0.0059	0.0041	0.0003	-0.0038
1958-1959	0.0405	-0.0020	0.0000	0.0012
1959-1960	-0.0028	-0.0052	-0.0007	-0.0037
1960-1961	0.0246	0.0004	-0.0001	0.0008
1961-1962	0.0241	-0.0027	-0.0004	0.0005
1962-1963	0.0301	-0.0013	0.0000	0.0006
1963-1964	0.0238	-0.0018	-0.0001	0.0007
1964-1965	0.0183	-0.0026	0.0009	0.0011
1965-1966	0.0096	-0.0020	0.0007	0.0013
1966-1967	-0.0059	-0.0017	0.0001	-0.0010
1967-1968	0.0170	-0.0039	-0.0000	0.0007
1968-1969	-0.0036	-0.0020	0.0001	0.0014
1969-1970	-0.0134	0.0001	0.0013	-0.0041
1970-1971	0.0244	-0.0002	0.0008	0.0033
1971-1972	0.0281	-0.0011	0.0016	0.0006
1972-1973	-0.0197	0.0132	0.0005	0.0026
1973-1974	-0.0698	0.0109	0.0006	0.0025
1974-1975	-0.0016	0.0047	0.0013	-0.0063
1975-1976	0.0375	-0.0019	0.0005	0.0004

tially offset by the largest positive contribution of the reallocation of value added during the period and smaller positive contributions of the reallocation of capital and labor inputs. The positive contributions of all three reallocation terms continued into 1974 as the weighted sum of sectoral rates of technical change dropped to 6.98 percent, a drop of more than 5 percent from the previous low in 1973. The negative weighted sum of rates of sectoral technical change continued into 1975, augmented by the negative impact of the reallocation of labor input and diminished by positive impacts of the reallocation of value added and capital input, resulting in a negative rate of aggregate technical change. Reallocations were negligible in 1976 relative to the sharp impact of a positive weighted sum of rates of sectoral technical change.

4.8. CONCLUSION

We have analyzed the role of capital in the U.S. economy over the period 1948-1976 on the basis of annual data from an aggregate production account in current and constant prices. In this concluding section, we summarize these data for the period as a whole and for the following seven subperiods: 1948-1953, 1953-1957, 1957-1960, 1960-1966, 1966-1969, 1969-1973, and 1973-1976. We present average rates of growth for the period 1948-1976 and for the seven subperiods in Table 4.6. The first part of this table provides data on growth in output and inputs from Table 4.2. The second part gives the contributions of capital and labor inputs to the growth of output from Table 4.3. The third part presents a decomposition of the growth of capital input and its contribution into components associated with capital quality and capital stock from Table 4.4. The final part contains a decomposition of the rate of aggregate technical change based on data from Table 4.5.

For the period 1948-1976, aggregate value added grows at 3.50 percent while capital input grows at 4.01 percent, indicating that the ratio of capital to output has risen during the postwar period. By contrast, labor input grows at only 1.28 percent, while the rate of aggregate technical change is 1.14 percent. The average rate of growth of value added reached its maximum at 4.83 percent during the period 1960-1966 and grew at only 0.89 percent during the recession and partial recovery of 1973-1976. The growth of capital input was more even, exceeding 5 percent in 1948-1953 and 1966-1969 and falling to 3.12 percent in 1973-1976. The growth of labor input reached its maximum in the period 1960-1966 and fell to 0.58 percent in 1973-1976, which was above the minimum growth rate of 0.23 percent in the period 1953-1957. Finally, the rate of technical change was a maximum from 1960 to 1966 at 2.11 percent. During the following period, 1966-1969, the rate of technical change was almost negligible at 0.04 percent. The rate of technical change recovered during 1969-1973, rising to 0.95 percent; finally, the rate of technical change fell to a negative 0.70 percent during 1973-1976.

Table 4.6. Summary

	1948–1976	1948–1953	1953–1957	1957–1960	1960–1966	1966–1969	1969–1973	1973–1976
Growth								
Growth in value added	0.0350	0.0457	0.0313	0.0279	0.0483	0.0324	0.0324	0.0089
Growth in capital input	0.0401	0.0507	0.0393	0.0274	0.0376	0.0506	0.0396	0.0312
Growth in labor input	0.0128	0.0160	0.0023	0.0099	0.0199	0.0185	0.0116	0.0058
Rate of technical change	0.0114	0.0166	0.0146	0.0113	0.0211	0.0004	0.0095	−0.0070
Contribution								
Contribution of capital input	0.0161	0.0194	.0154	0.0109	0.0156	0.0211	0.0161	0.0126
Contribution of labor input	0.0075	0.0097	0.0013	0.0057	0.0116	0.0108	0.0068	0.0033
Capital								
Growth in capital quality	0.0132	0.0206	0.0136	0.0080	0.0121	0.0172	0.0107	0.0071
Growth in capital stock	0.0269	0.0301	0.0257	0.0193	0.0255	0.0334	0.0288	0.0242
Contribution of capital quality	0.0053	0.0079	0.0053	0.0032	0.0050	0.0072	0.0044	0.0028
Contribution of capital stock	0.0108	0.0115	0.0101	0.0077	0.0106	0.0139	0.0118	0.0097
Reallocation								
Sectoral rates of technical change	0.0124	0.0219	0.0177	0.0145	0.0217	0.0025	0.0048	−0.0113
Reallocation of value added	−0.0016	−0.0075	−0.0030	−0.0010	−0.0016	−0.0025	0.0030	0.0046
Reallocation of capital input	0.0008	0.0022	0.0008	−0.0001	0.0002	0.0001	0.0010	0.0008
Reallocation of labor input	−0.0002	−0.0000	−0.0008	−0.0021	0.0008	0.0004	0.0006	−0.0011

To provide additional perspective on the sources of U.S. economic growth, we next analyze the contributions of capital and labor inputs to the growth of value added. Since the average value share of capital input is very stable over the period 1948-1976, the movements of these contributions among subperiods largely parallel those of the rates of growth of capital and labor inputs. For the period 1948-1976, the contribution of capital input of 1.61 percent is the most important source of growth in aggregate value added. The rate of technical change is the next most important source at 1.14 percent, while the contribution of labor input is the third most important at 0.75 percent. For the seven subperiods, the contribution of capital input is the most important source of growth during five subperiods, 1948-1953, 1953-1957, 1966-1969, 1969-1973, and 1973-1976. The rate of technical change is the most important source during two subperiods, 1957-1960 and 1960-1966.

Our first conclusion is that the contribution of capital input is the most important source of growth in aggregate value added during the period 1948-1976.[2] This conclusion is supported by our analysis of growth for the period as a whole, for the data by subperiods given in Table 4.6, and for the annual data presented in Table 4.3. An important key to revival of trends in U.S. economic growth established during the period from 1948 to 1966 is stimulation of the growth of capital input through capital formation.

To analyze the contribution of capital input to growth in aggregate value added in more detail, we can decompose the rate of growth of capital input into components associated with capital stock and the quality of capital stock. For the period 1948-1976, growth in capital stock accounts for two-thirds of growth in capital input, while growth in the quality of capital stock accounts for one-third of growth in capital input. This quantitative relationship between growth in capital stock and growth in capital quality characterizes most of the postwar period. There is a gradual reduction in the role of growth in capital quality in 1970-1973 and again in 1973-1976. These general conclusions hold for the growth rates of capital stock and capital quality and for the contributions of these two components in the contribution of capital input.

The decline in the rate of growth of aggregate value added from 1960-1966 to 1966-1969 resulted from a dramatic fall in the rate of aggregate technical change during those two periods. The growth of capital input actually increased, while the growth of labor input declined only slightly. The revival of growth in the level of technology during 1969-1973 was offset by declines in the growth of capital and labor inputs, leaving the rate of growth of value added unchanged. The rate of technical change became negative during the recession period 1973-1976. Our second conclusion is that a restoration of the rapid growth that characterized the U.S. economy from 1948 to 1966 will also require accelerated growth in the level of technology. This conclusion is supported by the evidence for subperiods given in Table 4.6 and the data on annual rates of technical change presented in Table 4.3.

We find it useful to decompose the rate of aggregate technical change into four components associated with a weighted sum of rates of sectoral technical change and with reallocations of value added, capital input, and labor input. For the period 1948–1976, sectoral rates of technical change account for almost all of the rate of aggregate technical change. The reallocation of value added is a negative 0.16 percent, while reallocations of capital and labor inputs are a positive 0.08 percent and a negative 0.02 percent, respectively. The collapse in the rate of aggregate technical change after 1966 resulted from a drop in the weighted sum of sectoral rates of technical change from 2.17 percent in 1960–1966 to 0.25 percent in 1966–1969. During 1969–1973, sectoral rates of technical change recovered to 0.48 percent; the most important contribution to the revival of the rate of aggregate technical change between those two periods resulted from the change in the reallocation of value added from a negative 0.25 percent in 1966–1969 to a positive 0.30 percent in 1969–1973. During 1973–1976, the weighted sum of sectoral rates of technical change declined to a negative 1.13 percent. The overall conclusion of our analysis of the rate of aggregate technical change is that accelerated growth in the level of technology for the U.S. economy as a whole will require greatly accelerated growth in the levels of technology at the sectoral level.

To provide a summary of our findings on the decline in the U.S. economic growth during the past decade, we can observe that this decline took place in two steps. First, the rate of technical change essentially disappeared as a source of economic growth after 1966. This can be traced to a very sizable decline in rates of sectoral technical change that began in 1966–1969 and persisted through 1969–1973. Second, in the period 1973–1976, rates of sectoral technical change nose-dived, beginning with a severe decline in 1973, followed by a catastrophic fall in 1974, and continuing with a further decline in 1975. The recovery beginning in 1976 was insufficient to restore levels of technology that had prevailed before 1973. We can also note that the recession of 1973 was greatly aggravated by a sizable drop in the rate of growth of capital input.

The prospects for future U.S. economic growth depend on the revival of growth in capital input that characterized the period from 1948 to 1973. The economic policies to stimulate capital formation adopted during the first half of the 1960s were highly successful in stimulating growth of capital input. New policy measures to stimulate capital formation can be designed on the basis of a wide range of past experience with incentives to invest. Future growth prospects will also depend on the resuscitation of improvements in the level of technology that characterized the period from 1948 to 1966. The fall in the rate of technical change after 1966 was severely aggravated by the further decline that began in 1973. Measures to stimulate the development and implementation of new technology at the level of individual industrial sectors must be designed and adopted. This task has no precedent in U.S. economic policy and poses the central problem facing policymakers of the 1980s.

NOTES

1. This paper is a condensed version of a more extensive study by Fraumeni and Jorgenson (1980). Detailed references to the literature are given by Fraumeni and Jorgenson (1980) and by Jorgenson (1980). Financial support from the American Council on Life Insurance and helpful advice from George M. von Furstenberg are gratefully acknowledged. We thank Nelda Hoxie, Helen Lau, and Betsy Rossen for their expert research assistance. Any remaining deficiencies are the responsibility of the authors.
2. This conclusion contrasts sharply with that of Denison (1979). For a comparison of our methodology with that of Denison, see Jorgenson and Griliches (1972).

REFERENCES

Christensen, Laurits R., and Dale W. Jorgenson, 1973, "Measuring the Performance of the Private Sector of the U.S. Economy, 1929-1969," in *Measuring Economic and Social Performance,* edited by Milton Ross, New York: National Bureau of Economic Research.

_____, 1970, "U.S. Real Product and Real Factor Input, 1929-1967," *Review of Income and Wealth,* series 16, no. 1, March, pp. 19-50.

Denison, Edward F., 1979, *Accounting for Slower Economic Growth,* Washington D.C.: Brookings.

Fraumeni, Barbara M., and Dale W. Jorgenson, 1980, "The Role of Capital in U.S. Economic Growth," in *Capital, Efficiency and Growth,* edited by George M. von Furstenberg, Cambridge, Mass.: Ballinger Publishing.

Gollop, Frank M., and Dale W. Jorgenson, 1980, "U.S. Productivity Growth by Industry, 1947-1973," in *New Developments in Productivity Measurement,* edited by John W. Kendrick and Beatrice Vaccara, Chicago: University of Chicago Press.

Jorgenson, Dale W., 1980, "Accounting for Capital," in *Capital, Efficiency and Growth,* edited by George M. von Furstenberg, Cambridge, Mass.: Ballinger Publishing.

Jorgenson, Dale W., and Zvi Griliches, 1972, "Issues in Growth Accounting: A Reply to Edward F. Denison," *Survey of Current Business,* vol. 52, no. 5, May, Part 2, pp. 65–94.

Kuznets, Simon, 1961, *Capital in the American Economy,* Princeton, N.J.: Princeton University Press.

5 PRODUCTIVITY CHANGE AS A FUNCTION OF VARIATION IN MICROECONOMY

Seymour Melman

5.1. INTRODUCTION

Productivity, as output per worker-hour, is rarely a primary objective for the decisionmakers of industrial or other enterprises. The measurement of physical output in relation to input is not one of the optimization criteria that are used by managers for assessing the performance of an enterprise. There is no productivity line in the traditional profit-and-loss and balance-sheet statements. However, productivity is of interest to the managers of enterprise and to trade unions, especially as they seek to escape the limitations of monetary measures for gauging the efficiency of particular aspects of enterprise performance, of sections of manufacturing operations, or of particular work operations.[1]

At the same time, the productivity of large aggregates, like single industries (or manufacturing, agriculture, and mining as a whole), has been of continuing interest to engineers and economists, since the levels and changes in physical output in relation to labor (or material or energy) inputs have a controlling effect on the sheer per capita quantity of goods that an economy is capable of deploying from its own production. Also, aggregate productivity measures denote average conditions for assessing the comparative performance of particular industrial subunits.

71

What is the linkage between productivity in large industrial aggregates and productivity in micro-units, such as single firms or plants, where the productivity criterion is only occasionally used as an explicit unit of measurement? Productivity is affected by every aspect of industrial production, ranging from work processes to quality of raw materials, climate, nutrition, the skills of workers and engineers, education, and the interpersonal style of managers. Nevertheless, some factors are much more important than others and dominate the scene. Thus the fivefold increase in output per worker-hour from 1900 to the present day in American manufacturing industry is associated with a host of alterations at the point of production. These alterations include, centrally, dramatic mechanization of the work processes and systematization of the organization of work. Wide application of changes in the methods and organization of production is the linkage between decision processes at the micro level that govern the selection of means of production and the macro effects of average output per worker that are of interest to economists and wider publics.

Since the Industrial Revolution of the eighteenth century in western Europe, industrial engineers and managers have had an array of alternative technologies (tools, machines, processes) for accomplishing a work task. Thereby the improvement in average output per man-hour worked can be linked to decisions by managers to move from one available method of work performance to another. For example, in a particular array of alternative methods for doing a commonplace materials-handling task, the current range of output per worker-hour is 9 to 1; that is, the most mechanized of the available array of methods will perform nine times as much materials handling per man-hour worked as is performable with the least mechanized array of methods.[2] A similar array of alternative methods is available for removing metal by lathes of various classes. The productivity range extends from 2.5 to 1. Finally, in the case of a measuring operation, the range of achievable productivity is in the order of 10 to 1 (Melman, 1956, pp. 12–15). These illustrations reflect magnitudes of productivity differences that are characteristically achievable in an indefinitely large number of industrial tasks.[3]

Since large changes in the productivity of labor are associated with changes in production methods, the issue arises: What decision mechanisms control the movement among the array of alternative production methods? It is beyond dispute that alternative tools, machines, and processes cannot activate themselves and cannot supplant each other; the means of production are inanimate things and have no volition. The decision to change means of production is in all cases a human decision and is made in accordance with the socially approved, mainly economic criteria and procedures that comprise the rules of microeconomy by which enterprises are operated. (The design of particular means of production is similarly governed, within constraints set by nature—the characteristics of materials, etc.)

Theoretically, an indefinitely large array of methods of decision making is applicable to this choice. Thus the variants include the following: who decides; the procedures of deciding; the criteria of optimization in deciding; the time-span effect of decisions; external constraints on decisionmakers; the relationship between those who decide and those who implement (separate groups, as in hierarchical systems, or the same people, as in cooperatively controlled enterprises). But the modes of decision making that are particularly relevant for this discussion are those of industrial capitalism.

In this view of the matter, productivity in U.S. industry appears as a derived effect of the operation of the industrial capitalist microeconomy. Hence the decision rules of that kind of microeconomy have special interest as factors governing productivity levels and productivity change. While this interest limits the alternatives that are considered here, it also facilitates an appeal to the facts of the case. Thereby decision-making alternatives in the microeconomy can be examined in terms of their bearing on the productivity of U.S. industry.

To address this matter, I present here three principal models that are used in the U.S. industrial economy for decision making on production methods: the cost-minimizing enterprise, the cost-maximizing enterprise, and the cost pass-along enterprise.

5.2. COST MINIMIZING

A crucial element of the microeconomy of the cost-minimizing industrial firm is the tendency for the degree of change in workers' wages to be characteristically greater through time than the degree of change in the prices of machinery purchased by the firm. In consequence, there is a systematic pattern of changes in costs of production to the firm that takes the form shown in Figure 5.1.

Unit costs in relation to the quantity of work done per day are shown here for a particular work operation. Costs are depicted for two production methods—one, highly manual in character, and a second, machine-using. At a given time, the cost per unit òf work performance by primarily manual means is the same over a range of output per day since unit costs by a manual method are dominated by the wages of labor, which are constant per unit of work, independently of the quantity of work done.

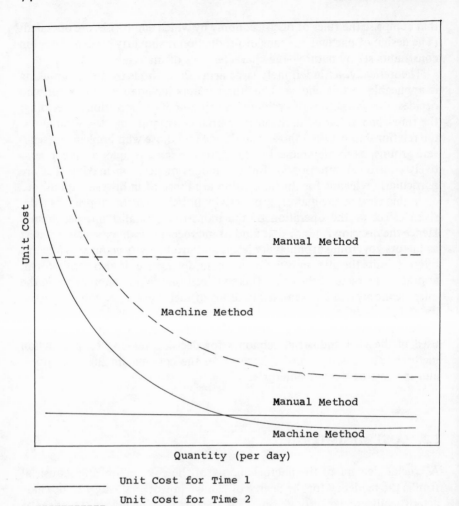

FIGURE 5.1. Alternative Labor and Machinery Costs under Cost Minimizing

In the case of the machine method, a small quantity of work done per day bears the burden of a fixed machine (amortization) charge per day, causing a high cost per unit at the low end of quantity. That cost per unit diminishes for larger quantities of work done per day. And so, as Figure 5.1 suggests, at some point in the range of quantity performance per day, there is a bit of calculable advantage in the machine method as opposed to the manual method.

However, the special character of the cost-minimizing model is visible in the cost behavior through time of machine-using versus labor-intensive work methods. Average hourly earnings to workers rise sharply, while prices of machinery increase much less rapidly. As a result, the cost per unit of work by machine method at time 2 is appreciably less than the cost of production by manual methods. That large unit-cost advantage appears over the greater part of the range of possible outputs per day. When the cost advantage associated with machine methods is so large as to offer the reasonable prospect of a payback on investment within five years or less, it serves as a decisive inducement to cost-minimizing managers to install and to use more machine-intensive work methods.

In this way, as the cost-minimizing enterprise addresses itself to minimizing the costs of production, it prefers the further mechanization of work. A sharp improvement in productivity is one derived effect of the cost-minimizing preference.

In this sequence of events, it is clear that a critical role is played by the greater degree of growth in the wages of labor vis-à-vis machinery prices. How can this happen? How can wages of labor rise more rapidly than the price of machinery? As the cost-minimizing managers of machine-producing firms are confronted with higher wage costs, they too are pressed to seek out less labor-intensive alternatives for getting their work done. Ignoring such options would leave them open to the risk of being noncompetitive. On the other hand, the consequence of seeking out and utilizing machines and methods that raise productivity in their own operations, thus offsetting all or part of cost increases, permits the machinery-producing management either to make no price increase at all or to increase their (machinery) prices less than the rise in wage costs would require. Therefore machinery prices appear progressively more advantageous to machine-using firms as an alternative to the prices of labor-intensive work methods, as depicted in Figure 5.1.

This effect is central to the operation of a cost-minimizing micro-economy and is due to the operation of the cost-minimizing mechanism within the machinery-manufacturing firms themselves. Thereby the machinery-producing industries play a critical role in further mechanization of work and in the productivity process.

What is the evidence of this process in operation? In the machine tool industry of the United States from 1939 to 1947, prices of machines rose 39 percent on the average, while average hourly earnings of industrial workers in manufacturing rose 95 percent. The rise in wages was 243 percent of the rise in price of machinery (Melman, 1958, p. 152). Cost analyses for particular work operations for the period 1939–1950 display precisely the sort of model behavior that is portrayed in Figure 5.1 (Melman, 1956, Chapters 6, 15). Thus in one materials-handling operation the wages of labor rose 6.7 times more rapidly than the price of the alternative equipment. It was precisely in that period, 1939–1950, that there was a very marked mechanization of materials-handling and allied operations.

What are the consequences for productivity from the thoroughgoing operation of a cost-minimizing microeconomy? The cost-minimizing criterion induces managers to change production methods in favor of further mechanization and systematization of work. The derived effect is the attainment of productivity gains systemwide.

As productivity gains occur for many firms, owing to progressive mechanization of work, the firms group themselves in a range around possible, achievable levels of productivity. Those enterprises that operate with internal stability of operation achieve a level of productivity that is optimum for particular machinery and tools; enterprises similarly equipped that function in an internally unstable manner achieve lower levels of productivity than the former (Melman, 1958).

Accordingly, the mechanization of work defines the central tendency of productivity growth for aggregates of plants or firms, and around that central tendency firms group themselves at a given time in accordance with diverse organizational and related features of their operations that affect stability of operations.

5.3. COST MAXIMIZING

A second form of microeconomy within contemporary U.S. industrial capitalism is characterized by cost maximizing. This feature appears mainly (but no longer solely) in the military microeconomy as an accompaniment to government-controlled subsidy maximizing.[4] Neither cost nor subsidy maximizing proceeds without limits. These interdependent processes operate under the constraint of public political decisions that determine the quantity of public money budgeted for offsetting cost increases in military and other subsidized activities.

In American experience, cost maximizing is a defining character of the internal economy of military industry, with 23,000 prime contractors; certain public utilities; and, as a recent study shows, certain hospital operations (Ihtiyaroglu, 1979).

In the U.S. military economy, the main buyer (the Department of Defense) is also functionally the top management of the military-serving firms (contractors). Through an elaborate system of product specification and controls over the interval functioning of the military-industry firms, product (including machinery) specifications are refined to deliver ever more exacting performance, the better to yield superior capability weapon by weapon compared with Soviet or other competition. Improvement of single weapons and weapon systems has been widely accepted as a big strategy for achieving the priceless state of military superiority. In the name of defense, weapon features like speed, precision, reliability, and shock effect are refined, even as the costs of these refinements rise geometrically. That same cost increase justifies larger budgets and hence ever greater scope of activity for managers in the military-industry network at all levels.

As machinery-producing firms became participants in these processes, the cost and prices of their machinery products show the effects in the form of increases that are no problem to the subsidized military buyer, but that generate an altogether new framework of cost alternatives for the cost-minimizing enterprise.

A central characteristic of the cost-maximizing, subsidy-maximizing microeconomy is the tendency for prices of machinery to rise more rapidly than wages of labor. The effect on machinery-using firms is illustrated in Figure 5.2, which utilizes the mode of presentation employed in Figure 5.1. Under the condition of cost maximizing, the prices of machinery in time 2 rise more rapidly than the wages of labor; hence the unit cost of doing work by machine methods rises more rapidly than the cost of doing similar operations by manual methods.

What is the effect on the machinery-using firm? If the user is a cost maximizer, then further mechanization of work can still occur (indeed, can even be encouraged) because the larger cost increase occasioned by the introduction of machine methods is offset by available subsidies. In fact, that pattern has been repeatedly noted in firms of the aerospace industry. If, however, the machinery user is a cost-minimizing enterprise, then the effect of this development in the relative cost of doing work by machine rather than manual methods is definitely to slow down new equipment purchase. As the regime of cost maximizing takes hold in machinery-producing industries, customers who remain cost minimizers may be expected to purchase machinery from abroad. The latter step is usually taken with reluctance by machinery-using firms, owing to problems of replacement, servicing, spare parts, and the like.

It is instructive to see how these processes have been expressed in the vital machine tool industry. Product specifications by the Pentagon and by NASA typically lead to elaborate, more costly design. Thus, the machine tool industry, following instructions and with contract support from the Department of Defense, proceeded during the 1950s to design equipment

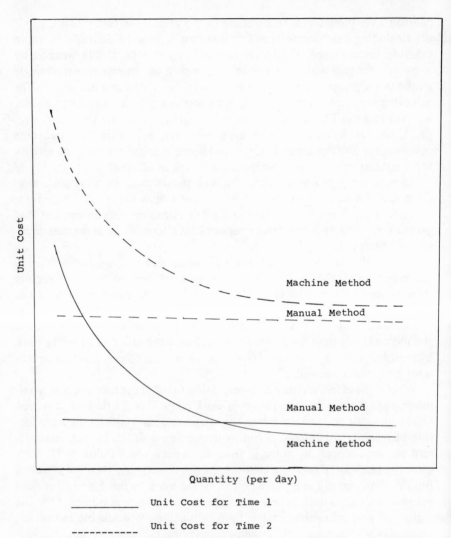

FIGURE 5.2. Alternative Labor and Machinery Costs under Cost Maximizing

with remarkably ornate control systems in response to such admonitions as "give the equipment maximum control capability." Thereby the cost of the control elements can be three times the ordinary cost of the main machine tool itself. Pentagon and NASA managerial procedures characteristically raise many classes of internal costs. Administrative costs are enlarged to unprecedented levels, both historically and by comparison with civilian-serving industry. Modes of production organization and cost computation that are favored have the effect of escalating production costs of all sorts. The resulting rise of machinery prices at a more rapid rate is not only an outcome of the pressures for cost increase (Boucher, 1981); it is facilitated and encouraged by the coexistence of a subsidy-maximizing system whose effect is to pay the higher price willingly.

The cost-maximizing practices introduced to important parts of the machinery-producing industries have checkmated the previous capability of those industries as suppliers of machinery at a historically lower rate of price growth as compared with wages of labor. Detailed evidence of this historic turnabout appears in the appendix to my volume *The Permanent War Economy,* where I list various machinery prices that in a recent decade increased more rapidly than wages of labor. Included are machine tools, construction equipment, and machinery in diverse other industries.

From 1940 to 1950, industrial wage costs (average hourly earnings) rose 121 percent, while machinery prices increased 22 percent. Hence, the wage cost increase to management was 5.5 times that of machinery. By contrast, from 1960 to 1970, U.S. industrial hourly earning rose 84 percent, while machine tool prices increased an average of 87 percent. The change in alternative cost of labor to machinery in the 1940–1950 period strongly favored the further mechanization of work. During the decade 1960–1970, this average impetus to mechanization was all but gone.

The effect of the change to cost maximizing within machinery-producing industries is also visible in efforts by leading firms of these industries to expand the military and the space market where subsidies are offered and in whose service internal cost maximizing can be accommodated.

The consequence for productivity is as follows: There is bound to be some growth in productivity in cost-maximizing firms insofar as they install equipment that, cost considerations aside, yields greater output per manhour. Thus, with high assurance, the installation of very complex (and remarkably expensive) multi-axis milling machines made it possible for milling-machine operators (plus programmers) to perform prodigies of work in shaping large structural members for high performance aircraft. There is no question that numerically controlled machine tools can perform that class of work with speed and precision no human operator can match.

However, the particular designs of numerical control equipment that were suitable for the Air Force's requirements were also so costly to purchase and to operate as to put this equipment well beyond the economic reach of most metal-working firms. One result has been that numerically controlled machine tools, after twenty years of active promotion, numbered about 2 percent of the U.S. machine tool stock by 1979.

At the same time, machinery-using firms that continued to operate in the microeconomy of cost minimizing responded to the unattractiveness of new machine tool prices by simply buying fewer of them. Replacement of older equipment was progressively deferred so that by 1973, 67 percent of the U.S. machine tool stock was ten years old and older. The United States was endowed with the oldest stock of metal-working machinery of any major industrial economy (*American Machinist,* 1973, p. 143).

5.4. COST PASS-ALONG

Finally, I take account of a third kind of microeconomy in U.S. industry and its effects on productivity, that of cost pass-along. Under this regime the firm maintains and improves its profit and other forms of advantage by responding to cost increases with the simple device of adding the cost increase (with appropriate overhead and profit margins) to price. Obviously, this pattern could not be workable if practiced by scattered single firms, since those firms, if not complete monopolies, would hazard loss of market share, and worse, if their competitors were meanwhile practicing cost minimizing and holding prices down. The evidence and analyses in hand strongly support a different view of the matter.

Following the sharp fall in productivity growth in U.S. manufacturing after 1965, the historic cost-minimizing process was disabled (BLS, 1971, p. 30). The growth in productivity was a principal means for offsetting cost increases from whatever source. In response to a new common situation, cost-minimizing managers discovered a common response: cost pass-along (Dumas, 1979; Hong, 1979).[5] As this new pattern became the modal condition of management behavior, its practice was no disadvantage to any single practitioner. Managers found that the former annoyed response among customers to price increases was replaced by resignation as customers learned that price increases and pass-along had become the new enveloping condition of business operations. Also, a diminishing cost-minimizing effort automatically entailed an easier life for managers. The work of revising production systems involves the redoing of work methods, equipment maintenance, production organization, wage systems, and the like. All such tasks in turn require changing the jobs of workers, engineers, and managers. The hard work and turmoil that is typical of efforts to offset cost increases is bypassed by the simplifying strategy of cost pass-along. Indeed, the former general practice of cost minimizing became so uncommon as to stand out whenever it appeared, as in the case of price decline, together with marked quality improvement, in hand-held and other calculators.

Independent, qualitative confirmation of the existence of this mechanism and of its extent comes from diverse data: from managements of various firms, from accountants with wide industrial experience, and from journalists who have inquired into the recent mode of operation of managers in various firms. (See, for example, *New York Times,* June 6, 1978, "Some Businesses are Hurt by Inflation, Others Benefit.")

Under the regime of cost pass-along, the rate of increase in wages to workers tends to be matched by the increase in prices of machinery. Why do the wages of labor and prices of machinery increase at similar rates under cost pass-along? The central feature of the enterprise operating under this form of microeconomy is retardation of productivity growth and hence of capability for cost offsetting. When this pattern becomes operative within the machinery-producing firms, then the prices of machinery (crucial costs to the rest of industry) are pressed upward in parallel with the growth of other prices. Seen through the eyes of the machinery-using firm, as in Figure 5.3, the resulting relationship between the costs of doing work by manual method and by machine method at time 1 are unaltered at time 2. There is no appearance of a cost advantage that favors the introduction of machine methods of work.

The conditions of cost-minimizing microeconomy clearly dominated in U.S. industry until 1965, and the machinery-producing industries had a key role in that process, for they had practiced cost minimizing within their own firms. What happened to alter this condition?

From the 1950s onward, the vital machine tool industry was brought into close relation with the Pentagon and its network of aerospace and other ordnance-producing industries. Parts of the managements and technical staffs of that industry became adept in the ways of cost maximizing. They also unlearned and replaced design and production practices and traditions that were integral to servicing a cost-minimizing microeconomy. As the technical and managerial base for cost minimizing was eroded within the machine tool industry, one net effect was that the average prices of metalworking machine tools increased by 116 percent from 1965 to 1977, equaling the rise of 115 percent of manufacturing hourly earnings for the same period (BLS, 1966, 1978). For the machinery-using firm, the effect of these developments is precisely the one that is portrayed in Figure 5.3: the virtual cancellation of cost advantage as an inducement to further mechanization of work.

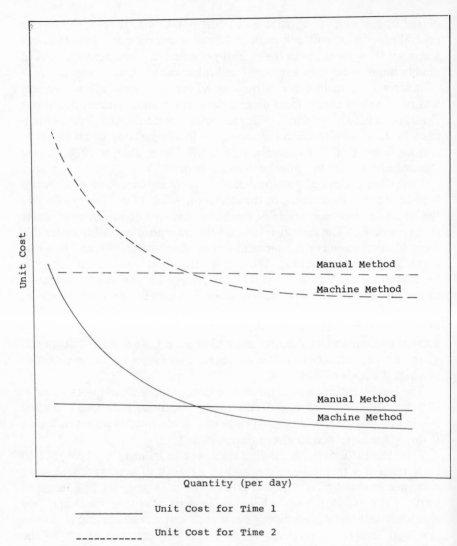

FIGURE 5.3.   Alternative Labor and Machinery Costs under Cost Pass-Along

Accordingly, the consequence for productivity from cost pass-along is to slow productivity growth by slowing the mechanization of work. From 1965 to 1970, the average annual change in output per man-hour in U.S. manufacturing was 2.1 percent; from 1970 to 1975, 1.8 percent. These were the lowest recorded rates of productivity growth for any western industrialized economy (BLS, 1971, p. 30).[6]

5.5. CONCLUSION

Three forms of microeconomy are now discernible in American industry. The pattern of cost minimizing had been the characteristic microeconomy of U.S. manufacturing firms. In the main, this has shifted to cost pass-along, with that microeconomy being the modal one since the mid-1960s. The U.S. industrial economy now includes a *cost-maximizing* sector that is dominated by 23,000 firms or major divisions of firms that serve the military economy.

With respect to impact on productivity growth, the controlling aspect of these microeconomies is their effect on the comparative change of labor (L) to machinery (M) costs. In summary, under cost minimizing, $\Delta L > \Delta M$; under cost maximizing, $\Delta L < \Delta M$; and under cost pass-along, $\Delta L = \Delta M$.

Inescapably, the shift from cost minimizing to cost pass-along plus cost maximizing must depress rates of productivity growth in manufacturing and other industries. The last two forms of microeconomy erode the classic cost incentive for mechanization and systematization of work that had long produced the U.S. pattern of productivity growth as a derived effect.

NOTES

1. When currency is unstable in value, many measures of output and input are flawed, thereby disabling money-valued productivity comparisons through time or between, say, comparable factories in different countries. Sharply rising costs of labor or energy will compel attention to optimizing output per unit of this sort. As changes are made in manufacturing equipment or in the organization of work, the proximate effects can be measured in the form of output/input of unit operations or of sections of a manufacturing (or other) system.

   Productivity measures are also used to support argumentation in collective bargaining with respect to work intensity and wage levels. The former lends itself to measurement within the limits of scientific competence of various measurement methods. See Abruzzi (1952) and Gomberg (1948). These books contain fundamental analyses of the problems of preparing reliable measures of industrial work. See also the relevant chapters in the standard handbooks of industrial engineering, for instance, Maynard (1974).

   As to productivity and wage levels, when the attempt is made to attribute a part of the money-valued product to any particular input factor, the issue becomes unresolvable as a scientific problem. While the *cost* of an input is known, it is altogether different to ask what has been the relative *contribution* (or *importance*) of each or any input factor to the money-valued product. Industrial output is typically the joint product of many inputs, all necessary; there is no way to determine how necessary any single factor may be since its withdrawal results in the cessation of all output. Bargaining decision power, or the relative social (market) valuation of an input, or both, remain the unavoidable final grounds for wage, salary, and other price determinations.

   For rapid access to a large literature on productivity, the reader can use the fine bibliographies, each titled "Productivity," compiled by the U.S. Bureau of Labor Statistics in its bulletins nos. 1514 (1966), 1776 (1973), and 1933 (1977). See also U.S. Bureau of Labor Statistics Report No. 559, *BLS Publications on Productivity and Technology,* 1979.

2. Such a ninefold difference in productivity should be understood as an average attainable difference across the range of alternatives. In each particular circumstance, the achieved productivity level is also affected by other variables: the mode of organization of work, the degree of alienation or disalienation of the work force, rates of absenteeism and turnover, and skill levels of the work force. The conditions of such variables can readily yield a variation of ± 15 percent around the average level of productivity that is attainable with particular equipment.

3. For twenty-five years, graduate students in industrial engineering at Columbia University have done exercises on productivity in relation to cost alternatives for work operations of their choice. The accumulated data for more than 500 tasks in numerous industries include the following features: In no instance has a work task been identified that lacks alternative methods (tool, machines, processes); typically, the range of available alternatives reflects large differences in productivity. A published example of these studies is available in Melman, Calderaro, and Suridis (1957). Scholars with a special interest in this file of data on alternatives in work operations should address this writer at the Department of Industrial Engineering and Operations Research, Columbia University, New York, N.Y. 10027.

4. A pioneering study in this field was carried out by Finger (1971). In it, he defined the reasons behind and the mode of operation of industrial subsidy systems as sponsored by governments. He found that within the framework of diversified grants to the firm from government, managers are powerfully motivated to enlarge costs since these form a major base for enlargement of subsidy requests. Government-based managers in turn use the cost maximizing of subsidized firms to justify the enlargement of their own budgets. Subsidy and cost maximizing are symbiotic processes: Each reinforces the other as managers in government and in firms fulfill their professional imperative to enlarge managerial control. See, especially, Finger's chapter "The Theory of the Subsidy Maximizing Firm."

5. I am satisfied that these studies and independent, confirming observations of a less systematic sort define a new cost pass-along microeconomy, but the exploration of these phenomena has hardly begun. At this writing, for example, there is no systematic formulation of criteria and units of measurement by which to define the extent or degree of cost pass-along within and among industries.

6. Data for 1970–1975 by special communication from the bureau. The three models discussed here represent three differentiated microeconomies; hence they are causal systems of three statistical "universes." As aggregation in productivity measurement encompasses firms representing more than one model, ambiguity attaches to the weight of each causal system in producing a measured aggregated "effect."

   There is no doubt that post-1965 productivity measurements for large aggregates like manufacturing as a whole include all three of the causal systems identified here. Therefore it is to be expected that measures of variability of factors held to be associated with productivity will be biased if the performance data of three differing causal systems are handled as though they are from one statistical universe.

   Inquiry into the details of the production functions that give rise to productivity variation must be specific to a particular "model" or causal system. Failing such differentiation, formally accurate statistical analyses for aggregates could reflect numerically correct mean values that actually represent bimodal or even trimodal distributions.

REFERENCES

Abruzzi, Adam, 1952, *Work Measurement,* New York: Columbia University Press.
American Machinist, October 29, 1973.
Boucher, Thomas O., 1981, "Technical Change, Capital Investment, and Productivity in U.S. Metalworking Industries," in *Aggregate and Industry-Level Productivity Analyses,* edited by A. Dogramaci and N. R. Adam, Boston: Martinus Nijhoff Publishing.
Dumas, L. J., 1979, "Productivity and the Roots of Stagflation," *Proceedings of the American Institute of Industrial Engineers.*
Finger, Nachum, 1971, *The Impact of Government Subsidies on Industrial Management,* New York: Praeger Publishers.
Gomberg, William, 1948, *A Trade Union Analysis of Time Study,* New York: Science Research Associates.
Hong, B., 1979, *Inflation under Cost Pass-Along Management,* New York: Praeger Publishers.
Ihtiyaroglu, Ibrahim, 1979, "Health Care under Cost Maximization," Ph.D. dissertation, School of Engineering, Columbia University.
Maynard, H. B., 1974, *Industrial Engineering Handbook,* New York: McGraw-Hill.
Melman, Seymour, 1958, *Decision Making and Productivity,* Oxford: Basil Blackwell; New York: John Wiley & Sons.
_____, 1956, *Dynamic Factors in Industrial Productivity,* Oxford: Basil Blackwell; New York: John Wiley & Sons.
Melman, Seymour, A. Calderaro, and J. Suridis, 1957, "Selective Studies in Alternative Man Hour Costs," *Journal of Industrial Economics,* July.
U.S. Bureau of Labor Statistics, 1979, *BLS Publications on Productivity and Technology,* Report No. 559, Washington, D.C.: U.S. Government Printing Office.
_____, 1978, *Monthly Labor Review,* January–June.
_____, 1977, Bulletin No. 1933, Washington, D.C.: U.S. Government Printing Office.
_____, 1973, Bulletin No. 1776, Washington, D.C.: U.S. Government Printing Office.
_____, 1971, *Productivity and the Economy,* Bulletin No. 1710, Washington, D.C.: U.S. Government Printing Office.
_____, 1966, Bulletin No. 1514, Washington, D.C.: U.S. Government Printing Office.

6 IMPROVING INDUSTRIAL PRODUCTIVITY AND TECHNOLOGICAL CAPABILITIES:
Needs, Problems, and Suggested Policies

Bela Gold

6.1. INTRODUCTION

There are very good reasons for the growing national concern in recent years about the decreasing rate of advances in the productivity and technological capabilities of wide sectors of industry. But these do not seem to be widely understood as yet. It is not surprising, therefore, that simplistic and erroneous diagnoses have encouraged support for ineffectual and even counterproductive policies.

The following analysis is based on extensive research on industrial productivity and technology in a variety of industries in the United States and overseas over a period of more than twenty-five years. Statistical studies at the level of individual industries have been supplemented with detailed examinations of operations at the level of single plants and even component departments in efforts to identify the factors shaping adjustments in performance.

As will be reviewed, key findings emphasize that productivity changes have generally been inadequately measured, that the relative importance of the factors affecting them has changed substantially since World War II, that such primary determinants differ among industries, and that the effects of productivity increases are often widely at variance with expectations. Misconceptions are also widespread concerning the risks and rewards of seeking to develop major technological advances and the rapidity with which successful innovations replace prior technologies. Even more important, however, is the basic conclusion that emerges: that diminishing rates of progress in the productivity and technological capabilities of major sectors of U.S. industry are attributable in greatest measure not to smugness, indifference, sloth, or ignorance, but to the absence of incentives attractive enough to offset the active deterrents to efforts to accelerate such improvements.

In order to clarify the analytical foundations for suggested policies to accelerate progress in industrial productivity and technological capabilities, the following discussion will first review the objectives of such policies and the sources and prospective effects of productivity and technological gains. This will be succeeded by examination of the considerations confronted by those deciding whether to increase or to decrease resource commitments to such improvement programs. The final focus will be on the policy implications of these various considerations.[1]

6.2. BASIC OBJECTIVES

The past twenty-five years have been characterized by an extraordinary upsurge of concern about productivity and technology. "Higher productivity" and "technological progress" have been widely regarded as equivalent to the magical Open Sesame formula for unlocking the storehouse of economic desiderata: more rapid growth, higher standards of living, improvements in the balance of trade, more leisure, and even inflation control. Such benefits could indeed result from advances in productivity and technology, but not without any accompanying costs and seldom without extended delays. Moreover, underlying such eventual global potentials, one must recognize an array of more specific and immediate effects that tend to be less universally welcome.

Improvements in productivity and in technological capabilities are primarily the result of decisions by particular groups, of course. And their decisions obviously tend to give much heavier weight to the specific criteria representing their own interests and responsibilities than to the amorphous aspirations of society at large. Accordingly, one set of useful insights into the causes of recent slowdowns in productivity increases and technological advances may be provided by considering differences in the evaluative profiles of the key groups influencing such decisions.

Actual changes in industrial productivity and technological capabilities take place in individual plants, and they are initiated by management decisions. In the private firms of the United States, the basic objective of such decisions is neither to increase productivity nor to improve technology, but rather to increase profitability. Profitability may be increased, however, through a variety of means, including improvements in product design, marketing, pricing, financing, and procurement. Hence, managements are likely to commit resources to programs for improving productivity or technology only up to whatever level seems to offer greater returns than these other alternatives relative to the costs, risks, and time delays involved. In short, managements are prepared to leave productivity levels unchanged, or even to reduce them, if that should appear to be more profitable—and this is often the case, as will be discussed later.

The next groups to be affected by managerial decisions involving changes in productivity and technology—and whose responses may react back on managerial evaluations—are the suppliers of the inputs involved, with labor usually the foremost. Their primary objectives tend to center around increasing wage rates, maintaining employment, improving fringe benefits, and reducing job hazards and discomforts. Because such goals may be promoted by some improvements in productivity and technology but undermined by others, members of the work forces affected and their trade unions may be much more favorable to some of these improvements than to others. And their responses to such innovations in the form of demands for accompanying adjustments in wage rates, employment levels, working conditions, and fringe benefits may significantly alter managerial evaluations of the prospective benefits of seeking to develop or to adopt particular improvements. Such decisions may also be influenced, of course, by the availability and prices of other inputs affected by particular innovations, especially capital. Even prospective adjustments in the availability and prices of particular materials and forms of energy may affect such managerial evaluations when such inputs are unusually scarce or under tight control by suppliers.

Consumers may also react more favorably to some improvements in productivity and technology than to others. They tend to applaud those yielding more durable, more service-free, safer, and lower priced products. But they are often less favorable to those that reduce variety in products responsive to wide differences in needs or tastes. In such product categories, management cannot help comparing the cost benefits of prospective innovations with possibly offsetting market penalties.

The most important of the remaining possible sources of influence on managerial decisions concerning possible improvements in productivity and technology is the government. Over the long run, the government seeks to promote a wide array of objectives, including reasonable economic growth, rising standards of living, the development and effective utilization of natural resources, the minimizing of involuntary unemployment, the maintenance of a strongly competitive position in international trade, and, of course, the safeguarding of the nation's military security. It is recognized that improvements in industrial productivity and technological capabilities may offer major contributions toward achieving such objectives. But it is also apparent that such improvements may entail negative effects on some of these objectives, at least in the short run and in some geographical areas and industrial sectors.

For example, some improvements in "productivity" may increase unemployment at their points of application. Some advances in technology may undermine the competitive position of older plants and older industrial areas and of smaller firms. Other technological innovations may increase demands for scarce resources or involve undesirable health, safety, and environmental effects. Thus, depending on their direct responsibilities, government agencies may differ widely in their enthusiasm for increasing productivity levels in various industrial settings and for accelerating the development and diffusion of particular types of technological advances.

But managerial decisions about innovations that may improve productivity levels and technological capabilities are likely to be affected even more directly by government policies affecting the prospective profitability of such undertakings. Among the most influential of these may be included tax policies, regulatory restrictions, and, in some industries, the prevention of unfair competition from foreign producers. It is therefore important to consider whether such policies, and especially recent modifications in them, have tended to encourage or to discourage greater managerial commitments to programs seeking to increase industrial productivity and technological capabilities.

Even this brief review would seem to demonstrate the existence of significant differences and even of some conflicts among the objectives of various groups capable of influencing the managerial decisions that largely determine the pace of productivity and technological changes in U.S. industries. Hence, any efforts to encourage acceleration of such advances would have to take account of the fact that this objective is not universally accepted and, therefore, that policies to promote it effectively must seek to minimize opposition while also increasing the incentives for prospective contributors to such gains.

6.3. NEEDED REVISIONS OF BASIC CONCEPTS

Changes in productivity levels are increasingly recognized as a major influence on a wide range of managerial problems, including wage levels,
cost-price relationships, capital investment requirements, labor utilization,
and even competitive standing. The very importance of these problems,
however, emphasizes the seriousness of continued widespread misunder-
standing of the nature and effects of productivity adjustments.

Among the most widely prevailing elements of the mythology relating to
productivity, the following five may be most important:

1. That productivity measures reflect changes in the "efficiency" of
    production;
2. That changes in productivity are reasonably well measured by output
    per man-hour;
3. That increases in output per man-hour or in output per unit of other
    inputs are invariably desirable because they yield decreases in unit
    costs and hence tend to increase profitability;
4. That cost-accounting analyses and management efforts to improve
    performance can be significantly improved by reliance on produc-
    tivity measures that purport to compare the quantity of all inputs
    combined with the quantity of all outputs combined;
5. That prevailing productivity measures permit reasonably effective
    comparisons of productivity performance among all firms within an
    industry and even among different industries, as well as comparisons
    with performance levels in the past.

And yet, not one of these beliefs is widely applicable even on theoretical,
much less on practical, grounds—as can readily be demonstrated.

6.3.1. Productivity and "Efficiency"

To begin with, it is inherently impossible to measure the physical "efficiency" of manufacturing processes or of most economic activities, for the
concept is based on a false analogy. To measure changes in the physical efficiency of a process requires comparing a combined physical measure of all
relevant inputs with a combined physical measure of all relevant outputs in
terms that reflect the primary purposes of the undertaking. Thus, one can
calculate an engine's physical efficiency *in respect to energy conversion* by

comparing the energy content of its fuel consumption with the energy equivalent of the useful power delivered by it. But it is not possible to measure the physical "efficiency" of the engine as a whole nor of the process of producing it. Such determinations are prevented by the absence of any important physical common denominators for combining the input contributions of labor energy and skills, many kinds of materials and supplies, even greater varieties of facilities and equipment, and a wide array of technical and managerial activities—in view of the obvious irrelevance of the available measures of numbers, volume, and weight. Nor are there important physical common denominators for combining the wide range of quality characteristics and service characteristics that differentiate the many available types of engines from one another.[2]

Lacking an economically significant concept of "physical efficiency," managerial efforts to improve operation must be refocused on appraising the effects of changes in various input-output relationships on specified performance objectives subject to management control. Thus, management needs a productivity analysis framework.

6.3.2. Labor or Other Inputs per Unit of Output as Productivity Measures

Outputs obviously represent the integrated contributions of numerous categories of purchased materials and supplies, various types of labor skills, many highly differentiated capital facilities and equipment, a wide array of technically specialized personnel, and a hierarchy of supervisory and other managerial contributions. Outside of service activities, labor inputs usually account for only a limited proportion of total input contributions, and hence changes in labor input requirements per unit of output tend to play only a modest role in accompanying output changes (for example, wages have long accounted for less than 20 percent of value of product in total U.S. manufacturing—although this ratio reaches 35 to 40 percent in some industries [Gold, 1971, pp. 137, 191]). Other inputs play comparably significant, but nevertheless limited, roles. Hence, management must be concerned with each category of input requirements per unit of output, while recognizing that the effects of changes in any category may change significantly over time and may differ widely among industries and even among firms in the same industry.

But it does *not* follow that decreases in any input per unit of output necessarily represent an increase in its productivity (i.e., its contributions to output per unit of input), or even that such a change is necessarily advantageous from management's point of view. Instead of reflecting an increase in a given factor's productivity, a decrease in its input per unit of output may result from shifting some of its former tasks to other inputs. For example, output per man-hour may rise for a variety of reasons other than increased efforts by direct labor: (1) It may actually result from a *reduction in labor's contributions through* the purchase of more highly fabricated components, the replacement of manual tasks by machinery, and the shifting of product-mix in favor of those requiring less manpower; and (2) it may result despite *no change in labor's contributions* through increasing the output of machinery without changing the numbers tending such equipment, either by utilizing machine capacity more fully or by increasing such capacity through technical improvements. Whether such reductions in any given input per unit of output are advantageous or not depends on their effects on total unit costs relative to the cost effects of the associated changes in the other inputs affected, and also on the effects of the given set of changes on the quality and revenue-producing potentials of the products affected by these productivity changes.

6.3.3. Unit Input Requirements, Unit Costs, and Profitability

The vulnerability of the expected advantages of increases in the apparent productivity of any given input is apparent from the uncertainty of its effects even on its own unit costs. The effect of changes in man-hours (or other input quantities) per unit of output on its unit cost depends, of course, on accompanying changes in wage rates (or in the relevant factor's price). Far from being independent of one another, as is assumed by common approaches to productivity analysis, changes in unit input requirements tend to *interact* with their factor prices. As a result, changes in the latter may either offset the expected unit cost saving, as in the common example of increases in wage rates paralleling gains in output per man-hour, or even accentuate such savings, as in cases where declining requirements for some materials may actually engender reductions in their prices.

In addition, the effects of such productivity adjustments on total unit costs also include the cost effects of changes in each of the other inputs affected by the given innovation. As a result, apparent increases in "productivity" often lead to increases rather than decreases in total unit costs. One of the most widespread examples of this involves the mechanization (or computerization) of manual tasks. Often, resulting increases in output per man-hour have not only been offset by accompanying increases in wage rates, thus eliminating the expected reduction in unit wage costs, but have also entailed increases in capital charges, thereby resulting in higher total unit costs than before the innovation.

The effect of apparent productivity improvements on profitability is not clear even in instances yielding actual reductions in total unit costs. Once again, one must examine not merely the changes in productivity relationships but also the specific means by which they were brought about. This is necessary partly in order to identify the possible changes already mentioned involving the relative contributions of different inputs and the relative mix of products. It is also necessary, however, in order to assess possible changes in the quality of products, which may affect the quantities that can be sold and the prices that can be obtained for them. And still another factor to be considered in estimating the prospective effects on profitability is the rate at which adoption of the same cost-saving innovation by competitors would tend to induce reductions in the market prices of the products affected.

6.3.4. On the Comparability of Productivity Measures

Changes in relative productivity levels are one of the most powerful sources of shifts in a firm's competitive position and also one of the most difficult to detect. Information about adjustments in competitors' product prices, input prices, marketing efforts, and investment commitments is usually readily obtainable. Nor is there much difficulty in identifying any significant changes in their products. Hence, reasonably good estimates can be made of the effect of such developments on a given firm's competitive position. Changes in the productivity relationships of competitors' internal operations, however, can seldom be estimated in most industries except within ranges too broad to offer effective bases for assessing recent modifications of relative competitiveness.

This informational gap may be costly not only because of resulting uncertainty about improvements in the performance of competitors but also because of management's accompanying inability to evaluate the satisfactoriness of performance within its own operations. For example, increases of 3 to 5 percent in some productivity relationships may be laudable or inadequate depending on the concurrent achievements of competitors.

Analysts have frequently placed heavy reliance on comparisons with industry-level data in appraising the performance of individual firms. Such expedients tend to be of dubious value in evaluating many aspects of performance, however, because of the heterogeneity of the operations encompassed by most of the industry categories for which statistics are published. These groupings have been devised by statistical agencies seeking to combine virtually innumerable dissimilar activities into a few hundred classifications differentiated from one another primarily on the basis of technology and of major product characteristics. Although such industry categories provide some useful insights into particular sectors within the economy as a whole, it should be recognized that most of them nevertheless encompass many forms of heterogeneity that may be especially significant for the evaluation of productivity relationships. These may include differences among reporting establishments in respect to product designs, product-mix, the scale and modernity of facilities and equipment, relative levels of fabrication of purchased materials, and rates of capacity utilization.

Accordingly, the value to any management of direct comparisons with group performance averages is determined primarily by the similarity of the operations included in the group, leaving the sheer size of the sample as a secondary, though obviously still significant, determinant of its usefulness. Thus, group averages for five to ten reasonably similar plants accounting for only 10 to 15 percent of the industry's total output may be far more valuable in assessing the comparative productivity performance of a plant like those included than would be data covering one hundred plants producing 85 percent of the industry's total output but also representing a wide range of heterogeneity in respect to the variables cited above. Nevertheless, valuable perspectives on comparative productivity performance may also be gained from group averages based on larger samples representing some decreases in homogeneity. For example, adjustments could be made to permit direct comparisons of productivity relationships despite differences in capacity utilization rates within the sample. Substantial differences in product designs, product-mix, the scale and modernity of facilities, and the relative levels of fabrication of purchased materials would obviously minimize the significance of direct comparisons of productivity levels. But as long as such differences among plants remain essentially unchanged—a situation not uncommon over periods of one to three years in many industries—valuable insights could still be provided by comparing *changes* in group averages with those of individual plants. This would be especially true when changes in the group averages are attributable primarily to the same factors that are affecting productivity adjustments in the plant being compared.

6.4. SOME SHORTCOMINGS OF COMMON PRODUCTIVITY MEASURES

Efforts to develop increasingly meaningful productivity measures seem to have resonated between overly fragmented and overly aggregated measures, instead of responding to management's need to understand the linkages between them as the basis for identifying the loci of gains and losses and thereby seeking to improve results.

There is little need for further discussion of the blatant inadequacies of output per man-hour as a measure of the productivity of total operations, although it may be worth emphasizing its unacceptability even as a measure of labor productivity in view of its lacking any consistent relationship to the magnitude or effectiveness of labor's contribution to the output representing the sum of all input contributions. What is less frequently recognized is the inadequacy of output per man-hour as a measure of productivity in service activities as well, unless output levels are overwhelmingly determined by labor inputs, unless each category of services is standardized in quality, and unless appropriate economic weights are used in combining different categories of service outputs as well as qualitatively different categories of labor inputs.

Other oversimplified measures that have been used in misconceived and vain efforts to measure changes in "efficiency," or "labor productivity," include the ratio of value added to man-hours or to total wage payments. Value added is, of course, merely the total value of products less the cost of materials, or the sum of wages, salaries, overhead, other costs, and profits. In view of the array of other factors affecting the inputs, costs, and revenues comprising the value-added numerator, it is obvious that increases in value added per man-hour need not have any consistently meaningful relationship to man-hours or total wage payments, as is implied by the terms *labor efficiency* or *total efficiency*. Indeed, inflationary increases in wage rates alone would tend to increase value added per man-hour. As for the ratio of value added to wage costs, this merely reflects the wage percentage of value added—another measure whose determinants include a wide variety of factors having no direct relationship to labor productivity or "efficiency."

It should also be noted that calculation of separate ratios of output per unit of various inputs may encourage misinterpretations. For example, the earlier cited example of mechanizing former manual tasks would result in increasing the ratio of output per man-hour and decreasing the ratio of output to capital investment. In fact, however, the actual innovation involves a partial shift in the tasks to be performed from labor to machinery. As a result, the actual contributions of labor to output per man-hour may have remained unchanged or may have even declined.[3]

Presumably because of the intuitive appeal of the concept of physical "efficiency" and of a single measure of changes in it, economists have developed an ostensible measure of changes in physical output per unit of all physical inputs, which involves dividing changes in product value at fixed product prices by accompanying changes in total costs at fixed factor prices. But how are resulting variations in this ratio to be interpreted? Do changes in product value (i.e., in total costs plus profits) at fixed product prices measure changes in total output or in total inputs? If the former, as has been suggested by Fabricant (1939), how are changes in total inputs to be measured? Application of the same approach would suggest measuring them in terms of changes in total costs at fixed factor prices, although differing conceptions of profit might suggest their inclusion or exclusion. But do changes in such ratios of total output to total inputs measure changes in "efficiency" levels (as implied by such terms as *total factor productivity* [e.g., Kendrick, 1961] and *aggregative efficiency index*, [e.g., Schmookler, 1952]), or changes in the ratio of (deflated) total revenue to (deflated) total costs—that is, some form of (deflated) profit margin—or changes in the ratio of product price to factor price indexes?

To answer these questions precisely, one should recognize that changes in these ratios may be due to variations in the quantity, price, or productive contribution of each specific input per unit of unchanged product; to differential changes between factor and product prices; to shifts in input factor proportions; and to fluctuations in the product composition of total output. Moreover, by applying fixed factor and product prices, this methodology tends to assume that there are no changes in the qualitative characteristics of materials, labor, capital goods, or products, although most substantial productivity changes are attributable to innovations involving just such qualitative changes in inputs, outputs, or both, especially over periods of several years or more. The assumption of fixed factor prices also implies that such prices are independent of the productivity adjustments being evaluated, instead of recognizing that the latter frequently interact with factor prices, as noted earlier. The resulting amalgam of interacting effects reaches far beyond the implications of any of the simple interpretations suggested above. Hence, such aggregative and hard-to-interpret results do not contribute much to management's primary objectives in developing the productivity foundations underlying cost accounting for the purpose of (1) identifying the changing input-output, factor-price, factor-mix, product-price, and product-mix relationships responsible for observed adjustments in various sectors of costs, and (2) using such findings as the basis for developing still more comprehensive performance evaluation and control measures, as well as better budget and planning estimates.

In view of the important role of technological innovations in changing productivity performance, it is also worth noting that the rich texture of technological effects cannot be encompassed by the crude economic tools developed during the many decades when the theoretical framework of economic analysis explicitly ignored such phenomena. Technological changes affect more than the quantities of inputs and outputs. Furthermore, estimated shifts in production functions, changes in the technical coefficients of input-output matrices, and deductions based on regression analyses offer unidimensional reflections of more complex relationships—and they accordingly offer estimates of resulting effects that are quantitatively subject to wide margins of error and that are often analytically meaningless.[4]

6.5. STRENGTHENING PRODUCTIVITY ANALYSIS

As noted earlier, advances in industrial productivity performance are determined primarily by decisions within individual firms and plants. Advances in productivity analysis can strengthen existing managerial guides for planning, controlling, and evaluating operating performance within the firm by providing deeper penetration into the sources of changes in costs, investment requirements, revenues, and profits. Such contributions require an analytical framework that would enable management to work backward from changes in the aggregate performance of the plant or firm to uncover the positive and negative contributions to that outcome of each organizational unit; to identify the productivity and other changes responsible for alterations in each unit's performance; and, furthermore, to determine the extent to which such changes were caused by departmental innovations vis-à-vis plant-level decisions, such as changes in product designs, product-mix, or capacity utilization. Such a framework would also facilitate working in the other direction to trace the effects of past or prospective productivity-improving innovations on inputs, processing methods, and product-mix through the successive linkages—from procurement through the various stages of production and distribution—that engender changes in overall operating performance and profitability.

To make such contributions practical as well as economical, productivity analysis must be broadened in coverage, integrated with existing information flows and control systems, and made applicable both to appraising the effects of prospective innovations in inputs or processes and to uncovering the specific causes of past adjustments in results.

6.5.1. Needed Coverage of Productivity Analysis

To fulfill the decision-making requirements of management, productivity analysis must reach beyond customary simplified approaches in order to cover:

1. Changes in the level of each category of input requirements per unit of output, including materials, facilities investment, and salaried inputs as well as direct labor;
2. Changes in the proportions in which inputs are combined, both in order to take account of substitutions (e.g., buying more highly fabricated components instead of making them, or replacing labor with machinery) and in order to differentiate between changes in the productivity of major vis-à-vis minor inputs;
3. Differences between the productivity of inputs when they are fully utilized and when their contributions are reduced by idleness (as, e.g., in the case of underutilized equipment);
4. Changes in input prices attributable to alterations in their quality as differentiated from changes in the prices of unchanged inputs;
5. Changes in the composition of output and in the relative prices of various products as differentiated from changes in the volume of output involving no significant shifts in product-mix;
6. Interactions among input volumes, qualities, and prices as well as among product volumes, relative prices, and mix;
7. Interactions between resulting changes in total unit costs, total revenues, and investment to determine effects on profit rates.

The following approach has been tested in a variety of applications over a period of years. Recently published accounts of such applications range from simple chemical processes (Eilon, Gold, and Soesan, 1976b) through progressively more complex electronics (Hildred, Nadler, and Bengston, 1978), glass (Skeddle, 1977), and metal-working operations (Eilon, Gold, and Soesan, 1976a) to a large integrated steel mill (Eilon, Gold, and Soesan, 1976a) and even the entire U.S. steel industry (Gold, 1976).

6.5.2. Productivity Measurement
Requirements

Merely comparing various input and output quantities reveals changes in ratios without indicating their significance. To make such findings meaningful requires an analytical framework that encompasses all of the inputs and outputs of the system and reveals how each contributes to overall performance. One could then work backward from specified performance objectives to identify the variables that affect them as well as intervening linkages.

The significance of given input/output ratios depends not only on the analytical relevance of the categories used, but also on five additional requirements whose intuitive recognition in simple production systems has often led to their being overlooked in other applications. Two of these concern the qualitative stability of each input and output category through time and their measurement in terms relevant to performance evaluation. The potentials for misinterpreting quantitative input/output changes when quality shifts are ignored may be illustrated by variations in such ratios for smelters, which may reflect variations in the metal content of ores rather than in smelter "productivity." And the dangers of measuring peripheral rather than core aspects of input and output flows may be illustrated by the common use of "tonnage shipped" to measure the output of steel mills, although most production efforts beyond the furnaces seek to increase the value of products by changing the shape, and incidentally reducing the weight, of the steel being processed.

The three remaining requirements are that the numerator and denominator of productivity ratios should relate to congruent sectors of activity, that they should relate to properly linked time periods, and that the contribution of the input must be absorbed into and affect the output. The first requirement merely seeks to prevent such errors as comparing all inputs of a plant with only part of its output (e.g., relating total man-hours in an integrated steel mill to the steel tonnage output of the furnaces). The second counsels against using input and output data for the same period unless all of the input is absorbed into the output within that period. Thus, in case of a six-month production cycle, output levels should be compared with material inputs six months earlier. The third requirement emphasizes that outputs should be compared with inputs of all factors that can be substituted for one another. Thus, changes in the ratio of pig iron input to steel furnace output would be misinterpreted if no account were taken of substitutions of scrap steel inputs in place of pig iron.

6.5.3. On the Productivity Network Approach

One means of meeting these needs is offered by the model depicted in Figure 6.1 covering direct inputs. It identifies six components of the "network of productivity relationships." Three cover the input requirements per unit of output, not only for labor but also for materials and fixed capital. In the case of the latter, net fixed investment is compared with productive capacity rather than with output in order to differentiate between what the capital goods can produce and the extent to which they are underutilized because of market factors (e.g., Gold, 1955, pp. 64–66). The remaining three links cover the proportions in which these are combined—for example, the extent to which more highly processed materials or additional facilities may be substituted for labor. Because of the possibility noted above that capital facilities may be underutilized, these factor proportions relate labor and materials inputs to "actively utilized" net fixed investment (Gold, 1955, p. 174).

By presenting productivity relationships as a network of interactions, this approach emphasizes that a change in any component, such as output per man-hour, may be merely the *passive* resultant of changes initiated elsewhere in the network, because all components must be brought back into a working balance. For example, the partial displacement of labor by additional machines would represent an initiating decrease in the ratio of manhours to actively utilized facilities and would lead to increased output per man-hour, even if the remaining labor continued to work at unchanged tasks and at an unchanged pace. But the adjustment process would not yet be complete. The increase in output per man-hour would require either a re-

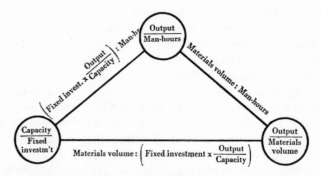

FIGURE 6.1.   The Network of Productivity Relationships among Direct Input Factors

duction in man-hours, if output remained at the earlier level, or an increase in materials inputs to permit the maintenance of total man-hours by increasing output in proportion to the gain in output per man-hour. In either case, the ratio of man-hours to materials inputs would decline, thus completing the adjustment cycle on the assumption that the originating replacement of labor by additional machines involved no change in materials requirements per unit of output or in the ratio of capacity to fixed investment (Gold, 1975*b*, pp. 13–14).

In short, in using this model of the network of productivity relationships, it is necessary to identify the source of the innovational impact instead of assuming that it was engendered within any component registering a change. It is also necessary to trace the effects of an initiating impact in any component through the adaptive adjustments necessitated in the other components of the integrated process.

6.5.4. Integrating Productivity Network Analysis into the Cost and Profit Analysis

Management cannot, however, evaluate the net benefits of a past or prospective innovation solely on the basis of adjustments in the six components of the network of physical productivity relationships. The analysis must be extended to include their economic effects if it is to serve as a sound basis for decisions. To explore the cost effects of changes in unit input requirements and factor proportions, one can superimpose the "structure of costs" onto the "network of productivity relationships" (Gold, 1955), as shown in Figure 6.2.

The effect of changes in output per man-hour on unit wage costs depends, of course, on concomitant changes in wage rates. Similarly, the effect of changes in unit material requirements on unit material cost depends on accompanying changes in the price of such materials. And the effect of changes in the productivity of fixed investment on capital charges per unit depends on the annual charges on such investment and on the capacity utilization rate. The point being emphasized in this framework is the necessity of considering *interactions* between productivity adjustments and factor prices instead of assuming that the latter remain unchanged.

In turn, the effect of a change in unit wage costs on total unit costs depends on the wage proportion of total costs, as well as on concomitant changes in other unit costs weighted by their respective shares of total costs. For example, if wages account for less than one-fifth of total costs, as is common in U.S. manufacturing (Gold, 1971, pp. 185–91), a 5 percent de-

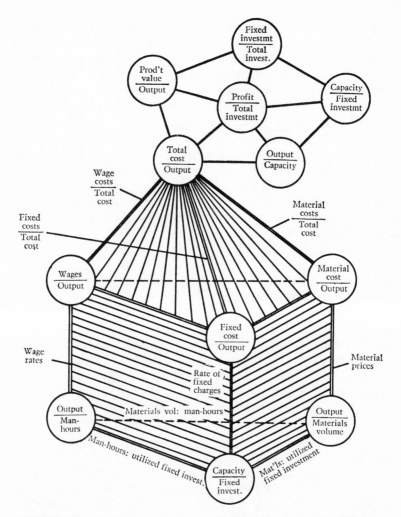

FIGURE 6.2 Productivity Network, Cost Structure, and Managerial Control Ratios

crease in unit wage costs would tend to reduce total unit costs by only 1 percent. But total unit costs are more likely to increase than decrease if the innovation engendering the decline in unit wage costs involved increases in unit material and unit capital costs, which together account for more than three times the wage share of total costs in many manufacturing industries (Gold, 1971, p. 137).

Integration of the productivity network and cost structure models thus relates changes in "apparent" input productivities and factor proportions through factor prices to each of the unit costs; it also relates changes in individual unit costs through cost proportions to total unit costs. Hence, it identifies the additional kinds of information required to evaluate the prospective effects on total unit cost of given patterns of past or anticipated changes in the network of productivity relationships.

It should also be recalled that analysis of the effects of productivity adjustments must begin by identifying their sources. Thus, labor-management disputes about the extent of increases in output man-hour and attendant adjustments in wage rates often divert attention from the means and costs of effecting the changes in output per man-hour.

Finally, managerial decisions in private industry obviously cannot be based on minimizing total unit cost either. Accordingly, the "productivity network" and the "structure of costs" must be further integrated with some model of the determinants of changes in profitability, such as the "managerial control ratios" shown in the top level of Figure 6.2. According to this system (Gold, 1971, Chapter 2), efforts to increase the rate of profits on total investment need not concentrate on cost-reducing innovations alone. Indeed, the latter would be deemed undesirable if achieved by means leading to reductions in product prices and capacity-utilization levels that more than offset the prospective gains in profitability derived from unit cost reductions. Conversely, innovations might be deemed attractive if they offer prospects of increases in capacity utilization and in product prices large enough to offset any increases in total unit cost (whether due to higher priced input factors or heavier input requirements per unit of output). Figure 6.2 illustrates such a unified framework for systematically exploring the interactions linking changes in factor inputs and factor prices to unit costs and cost proportions and to the other determinants of changes in the rate of profits on investment (Gold, 1971, Chapters 2 and 8).

The preceding model may also be disaggregated, of course, to permit progressively deeper penetration of plant operations in the interests of identifying the specific sources of changes observed at more aggregative levels or, alternatively, in the interests of more detailed exploration of the more aggregative effects of prospective productivity or technological changes in particular operations or departments. Thus, changes in the total unit costs of materials can be separated into the unit costs of each category of purchased materials, supplies, and energy. And each of these components of total unit material costs may then be decomposed into unit input quantities and their respective prices—tied into a productivity network in order to take account of possible substitutions among them. Total unit labor costs might similarly be separated into the unit costs of direct labor and those of indirect labor before further decomposition into their productivity network components. Capital investment may also be decomposed along parallel lines. The general process of elaborating the intraplant extension of the model is illustrated by Figure 6.3.

6.5.5. Productivity Changes beyond Plants and Firms

There has been an unfortunately widespread tendency in economics to project relationships that are meaningful at given levels of aggregation to other (usually higher) levels of aggregation where they are less meaningful and at times even misleading. Profits, for example, are directly meaningful only at the level of firms, for industry aggregates reflect some unknown combination of increases by some firms at the expense of others, yielding no homogeneous measure applicable to the industry as a whole. Such limitations are even more true of productivity measures, for these may differ widely among products and among plants as well as among firms. As a result, industry-level measures of changes in particular input/output ratios can seldom be soundly interpreted as measures of either the effects of particular innova-

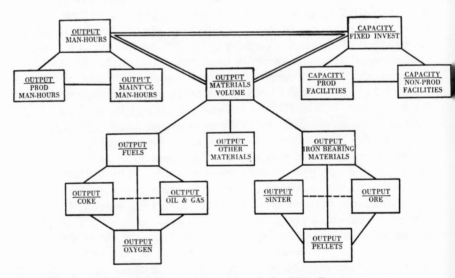

FIGURE 6.3.   Elaborated Productivity Network for Blast Furnaces

Source: Reprinted by permission of the publisher, from *Research, Technological Change, and Economic Analysis,* edited by Bela Gold (Lexington, Mass.: Lexington Books, D.C. Heath and Company, copyright 1977, D.C. Heath and Company).

tions or the causes of concomitant changes in costs. Indeed, they are usually vulnerable even as indicators of whether given developments were economically advantageous or disadvantageous.[5] Yet measures of this kind have often been used to evaluate industrywide wage claims, technological progressiveness relative to other industries and foreign competitors, and even the justifications for price increases.

It follows that commonly available productivity measures at even higher levels of aggregation tend to be still more vulnerable as additional heterogeneities—including differences among manufacturing industries and even wider disparities among other sectors of production—are swept under the rug of increasingly encompassing totals.[6] This does not mean that all aggregative measures are useless. Rather, it emphasizes that highly specialized measures must be used to serve various purposes, that some aspects of performance cannot be effectively measured at higher levels of aggregation,[7] and that it is hazardous to rely on simplistic measures in attempting serious evaluations of productivity performance at the level of industries and beyond.

6.6. PRIMARY SOURCES OF PRODUCTIVITY ADJUSTMENTS

Among the vast multiplicity of changes that affect actual industrial operations, eight major types may be selected as having a primary bearing on productivity levels. These are product design, product composition of output, the nature of production processes, the scope of fabrication or processing activities encompassed, the effectiveness with which operations are integrated, the productive capacity of operations, the degree of utilization of available capacity, and the nature of the inputs employed.

The categories most likely to account for long-term adjustments in productivity levels are advances in the nature of the processes employed; improvements in the effectiveness with which operations are integrated; increases in the scale of production; advances in the quality of inputs, especially of materials and capital; and changes in the scope of operations. Each of these is capable of engendering major adjustments in productivity levels—advances in integration and in the quality of inputs tending to be individually smaller, but also more continuous, than adjustments in the other categories. Moreover, each of these sources of long-term productivity adjustments tends to raise rather than to lower productivity levels, with the possible exception of adjustments in the scope of operations, which may involve shifts in either direction through "make-or-buy" decisions and those involving backward or forward integration.

The changes in industrial operations most likely to account for short-term variations in productivity levels are changes in the product composition of output; fluctuations in the rate of operations; adjustments in product design; changes in the quality of inputs, especially of labor and of materials; and advances in the effectiveness with which operations are integrated. All but the last of these categories may engender either increases or decreases in productivity levels during short periods. Among these categories of change in industrial operations, the greatest adjustments within short periods are likely to be those involving the product composition of output and the rate of operations, although abrupt changes may on occasion affect the quality of labor and material inputs as well. It should also be noted that most of these sources of short-term variations in productivity levels tend to affect the proportions in which factors are combined for the production operations as a whole, rather than altering the nature and efficiency with which individual tasks are performed. Surely, this tends to be true of changes in the product composition of output and in the rate of operations, the most influential of the categories reviewed.

Thus, over the long run, productivity levels may be expected to follow an upward trend, while productivity levels for entire production processes may be expected to fluctuate over the shorter run. It should be emphasized, however, that the latter result is less likely to involve changes in the efficiency with which individual production tasks are performed than changes in the incidence of idleness among the components of operations as a whole or changes in the product composition of output. Hence, the productivity of actively utilized inputs is more likely to rise than to decline even in the short run, except when extraordinary reductions in the quality of inputs must be absorbed or when major changes in the product composition of output are experienced by establishments whose product lines differ significantly in respect to their productivity levels or factor proportions.[8]

Of course, actual changes may represent the interaction of adjustments in each of several categories, thus requiring appraisal of simultaneous pressures in various directions. Even more important, it should be recognized that although these changes affect productivity levels, they may be attended by other effects as well and that from the standpoint of top management objectives, these other effects may be either more influential or less influential than the productivity effects. Hence, industrial operations may be changed in directions involving reductions in certain productivity measures, not only because of inescapable market pressures but also because of deliberate managerial efforts to advance other objectives of the enterprise.[9]

Changes in relative contributions to productivity adjustments may be illustrated by the remarkable reversal in the basic steel industry after 1947.

Because this is a "capital-dominated" industry, with labor's role largely restricted to tending equipment in accordance with technically determined procedures, changes in output per man-hour may be attributed overwhelmingly to changes in the productivity of capital facilities (as measured by productive capacity per dollar of net fixed investment) and to changes in the amount of such actively utilized facilities teamed with labor (as measured by net fixed investment—adjusted for capacity utilization rates—per man-hour). Between 1904 and 1947, an increase of 185 percent in the productivity of net fixed investment combined with an increase of 49 percent in actively utilized net fixed investment per man-hour to raise output per man-hour by 329 percent. Between 1947 and 1969, however, an increase of only 45 percent in output per man-hour was achieved by increasing actively utilized net fixed investment per man-hour by 165 percent to offset a 60 percent *decline* in the productivity of net fixed investment.[10]

As has already been noted, measures of apparent changes in factor proportions and in the productivity of individual inputs at successively more aggregative levels beyond the plant become increasingly difficult to interpret because of the expanding array of factors capable of influencing them. In the case of firm-level data covering multiple plants, such results would reflect any significant deviations from the past pattern of interplant differences in respect to each of the eight major types of changes in industrial operations reviewed above, thus requiring information about the past as well as the current status of each for every plant. In the case of industry-level data, similar information would be required not only for all plants and firms functioning in both the base and the comparison period but also for all plants added and eliminated since the base period. One need hardly add that these represent quite formidable requirements even without the further information needed for analyzing still more aggregative data.

6.7. EFFECTS OF CHANGES IN TECHNOLOGY AND PRODUCTIVITY RELATIONSHIPS

The effects of changes in technology and in productivity relationships are determined by a succession of decisions and interactions reaching outward from the plants immediately affected to their factor and product markets. The first of these involves management choices among alternative means of utilizing the potential benefits of a given improvement in factor proportions or in the productivity of a given factor. The next encompasses resulting interactions with factor prices. Further linkages of concern to management deal with the other determinants of profitability included in the model represented by Figure 6.2. Appraisal of prospective industry-level and still broader effects obviously requires consideration of a variety of other factors as well.

6.7.1. Constraints on the Harnessing of Productivity Adjustment Benefits

Two groups of factors tend to narrow the range of alternative allocations of given productivity adjustments: those tending to engender similar limitations in all industries and those tending to produce differing limitations among industries. The first group consists primarily of changes in productive capacity and in physical output; their effects center on the choice between expanding productive contributions or contracting the volume of inputs. The second group is rooted in the technological differences among industries; their effects center on alternative allocations of the effects of originating productivity adjustments between modifications in factor proportions and changes in the productivity of other direct input factors.

General Effects of Output and Capacity Adjustments. Increases in the productivity of labor in any industry might obviously be utilized either by reducing employment proportionately while maintaining output or by maintaining employment through expanding output proportionately. The former need not affect either product or factor markets, except for reducing demand for labor (unless this reduction were to encounter effective resistance). But output expansion would tend to affect product markets through the increased supply to be sold, as well as materials markets through the increased demand for such inputs. The increase in output would permit fuller utilization of capital facilities if they had been underutilized, but would require increases in investment if utilization levels were already optimal. Decreases in input requirements of materials per unit of output would tend to offer similar options to management, with similar repercussions in product and factor markets.

In theory, increases in the productivity of fixed capital inputs might likewise be absorbed either through an increase in productive capacity with no change in the level of investment or through keeping capacity unchanged by a proportionate reduction in the capital facilities and equipment embodying investment. But the latter option is seldom practical when the productivity gain results from technological advances that raise the productive capacity of the existing capital stock. In such cases, the durability and the specialized nature of a given plant's facilities may prevent any proportionate reduction in productive facilities and the investment embodied in them except over extended periods. This means that the benefits of increases in the productive capacity of existing capital facilities tend to be offset by decreases in its utilization rate to the extent that output expansion falls short of the gain in capacity. On the other hand, effecting such increases in output would tend to have carry-over effects on product markets and would also involve increased demand for materials inputs and perhaps for labor as well.[11]

It should also be noted that the above discussion of labor assumed that it is always capable of adjustment in direct proportion to changes in output. But such flexibility varies widely among industries, and hence the more limited such flexibility, the more relevant to the evaluation of management options would be the analysis presented for increases in the productivity of capital.[12]

Specialized Effects of Technological Differences. Attention may be turned now to the second source of constraints on managerial options concerning alternative allocations of the effects of given productivity adjustments: the technological nature of the basic processes involved. The aspect of the nature of production processes that seems to be of greater significance in the present connection concerns the comparative roles of direct labor, capital facilities, and direct materials in determining productive capacity.

Actual industrial processes cover a wide range in respect to the relative influence on productive capacity of changes in direct labor, capital facilities, and direct material inputs. One extreme might be characterized as "capital-dominated."[13] This category would include processes in which production workers are engaged overwhelmingly in starting, stopping, loading, unloading, setting controls, or otherwise simply facilitating the functioning of machines and other capital facilities. In this category, materials would play merely the passive role of providing the standardized inputs being acted upon by the machine process. Similarly, the "labor-dominated" extreme would encompass processes in which tools and other capital facilities serve essentially as accessories to wage earners whose manual efforts and related skills represent the fundamental core of the production process, materials once again serving passively as the standardized inputs being acted upon by manual operations. One may likewise envision a "materials-dominated" extreme covering operations in which productive capacity is dominated by the resources to which labor and capital facilities are applied, both of the latter merely facilitating attainment of the production capacity determined by materials and related inputs.

As is generally true of the enormous diversity to be found in the real world, these extremes may well prove to account for but a limited proportion of actual industrial operations. Nevertheless, a summary of the ways in which this classification of processes according to factor dominance tends to affect productivity relationships may shed some further light on the probable effects of productivity adjustments in particular situations.[14]

In operations approximating the capital-dominated extreme (e.g., power plants, cement mills, and blast furnaces), increases in labor productivity are more likely to reduce man-hour requirements than to increase productive capacity or the productivity of fixed capital; increases in the productivity of fixed capital are likely to leave direct labor requirements per unit of fixed capital input unchanged or reduced and hence to induce parallel increases in physical output per man-hour; and major advances in the productivity of the operation as a whole are thus much more likely to come from—and are better measured by—adjustments in the productivity of fixed capital than in the productivity of labor. In operations approximating the labor-dominated extreme (e.g., bricklaying, custom tailoring, and carpentry), increases in the productivity of fixed capital are more likely to reduce requirements for such equipment than to increase productive capacity or the productivity of direct labor; increases in labor productivity are likely to leave fixed capital requirements unchanged and hence to induce parallel increases in the productivity of fixed capital; and major advances in the apparent productivity of the operation as a whole are thus much more likely to come from—and are better measured by—adjustments in the productivity of direct labor than in the productivity of fixed capital.

Moreover, both in labor-dominated and in capital-dominated fabricating processes, materials requirements tend to vary with output levels, thus tending to increase the ratio of materials inputs to labor inputs with an increase in the productivity of labor and to increase the ratio of materials inputs to effectively utilized fixed capital inputs with an increase in the productivity of fixed capital. And in such processes, decreases in materials input requirements per unit of output are more likely to reduce the volume of materials input requirements than to increase the productivity of other factors or the productive capacity of the operation as a whole. Also, in both labor-dominated and capital-dominated extractive processes, changes in the richness of materials inputs may be a determinant of significant changes in the productivity of the process as a whole, tending to be reflected by increases in the apparent productivity of both labor and fixed capital.

In operations approximating the materials-dominated extreme (e.g., farming, fishing, and smelting), increases either in the productivity of direct labor or in the productivity of fixed capital are more likely to reduce requirements for such inputs than to increase productive capacity or the productivity of materials and related inputs. Also, increases in the productivity of these dominant resources are likely to leave labor and fixed capital requirements unchanged, thus inducing parallel increases in the productivity of direct labor and of fixed capital. Finally, major advances in the productivity of the operation as a whole are much more likely to come from—and can be better measured by—adjustments in the productivity of materials and related inputs than in the productivity of direct labor or of fixed capital.

In short, increases in physical output per man-hour are most likely to result from increases in the productive contributions of labor only in labor-dominated processes; in capital-dominated processes, such increases are more likely to be a reflection of gains in the productivity of fixed capital; and in materials-dominated process, such increases are more likely to be a reflection of gains in the productivity of natural resources and related inputs. Similarly, increases in the productivity of fixed capital are most likely to result from increases in the productive contributions of the investment embodied in capital facilities and equipment only in the case of capital-dominated processes; in other processes, such increases are more likely to be a reflection of gains in the productivity of the factor dominating the process. Increases in the productivity of materials and related inputs are in the same way most likely to result from increases in the productivity of these inputs only in materials-dominated processes.

Finally, it is useful to consider briefly how the generalized effects of output and capacity changes differ from the specialized effects of production processes in limiting managerial options in utilizing the effects of given productivity adjustments. In respect to the continuity of their effects through time, it is not only apparent that output tends to vary more in the short run than capacity, but also that capacity levels are more likely to change over somewhat longer periods than is the basic nature of productive processes. Accordingly, the influence exerted by initial output and capacity adjustments are likely to be less enduring than those engendered by the basic nature of productive processes. With respect to their susceptibility to managerial control, it is apparent that the basic nature of productive processes is less amenable to managerial manipulation than are output and capacity levels. Of course, output and capacity levels must be adjusted to market potentials and competitive forces. Nevertheless, sufficient uncertainty attends such estimates to allow considerable scope for the application of managerial preferences in many industries, especially over an extended period of time. On the other hand, the basic nature of productive processes tends to change but slowly, except under the stimulus of major technological advances, which tend to be uncommon.

6.7.2. Hypotheses concerning the Diffusion and Effects of Improvements in Productivity

Because of the meagerness so far of empirical samplings of the vast and complex terrain of technological and productivity advances,[15] few expectations can be regarded as authoritative. Our own extensive studies, however, seem to warrant hazarding the judgment that the following widely prevailing assumptions cannot be justified:[16]

1. That resource-saving (productivity-improving) innovations tend to yield comparable reductions in their respective unit costs;
2. That technological advances and associated productivity improvements generally reduce total unit costs and prices;
3. That technological innovations and associated productivity improvements tend to increase profitability either in the short run or over the long run;
4. That the benefits of technological innovations and of productivity improvements are most effectively measured by reductions in "real unit costs";
5. That even demonstrably superior technological innovations are, or should be, promptly adopted throughout an industry.

6.7.3. Some Implications of Altered Expectations

The apparent vulnerability of the above widely accepted assumptions or expectations concerning the effects of improvements in industrial productivity and technology should not discourage continued promotion of these major sources of economic and social progress. On the contrary, recognition of such limitations should help to prevent the potentially inhibitory effects of using inappropriate criteria to judge their results.

As a matter of fact, engineering estimates of changes in physical input requirements and output potentials are quite commonly confirmed, albeit often only after longer periods than expected. The burdens caused by decreasing supplies of high-grade raw materials have been largely offset in most cases. Pollution levels of most industrial plants have been substantially reduced. Labor requirements per unit of output have declined sharply, while hazardous and brutally arduous work has been increasingly displaced by tasks placing greater emphasis on skills and knowledge. Improved facilities, equipment, and instrumentation have made possible extraordinary advances in product capabilities, quality, and variety, as well as in productive capacity and in the precision with which operations could be adapted to changes in inputs, output levels, and product-mix.

Hence, the vulnerability of the above expectations was rooted in the assumption that economic benefits would directly parallel such physical improvements. Reliance on such assumptions, however, is evidence of a failure to supplement expert engineering evaluations of immediate physical readjustments with expert production management estimates of subsequent physical readjustments in associated sectors of operation and, far more important, with comparably expert economic analyses of the probable effects of the unavoidable interactions of both sets of physical readjustments with short-term and longer-term supply-and-demand pressures in input factor and product markets.[17] Such additional analyses would help to develop more realistic estimates of the magnitude and time patterns of the net benefits of alternative innovations, as well as of the advantages and disadvantages of pioneering versus following competitors. Moreover, such economic analyses may also contribute to the planning of future research and innovational efforts by identifying supply, demand, and price trends in factor and product markets that foreshadow developing pressures and opportunities.

Over the long run, survival requires keeping up with the technological progress of foreign as well as domestic competitors. Moreover, remaining competitive in the face of reductions in foreign trade barriers requires that domestic productivity levels surpass those of overseas producers by a margin sufficient to offset any of their advantages in respect to wage rates and other prices and qualities.

Finally, it should be emphasized that although the economic benefits of technological innovations that can be captured by individual firms tend to be smaller and shorter-lived than seems to be widely expected, such rewards may still compare favorably with alternative sources of differential advantages over competitors. And yet this raises the question of whether such incentives are large enough to encourage a level of investment in technological progress that accords with national social welfare objectives. After all, most of the benefits that flow through and then past the innovating firms and industries accrue to society at large in the form of higher real incomes per capita, more effective utilization of scarce resources, industries that are more competitive in domestic and world markets, less onerous work, and a generally stronger and more secure economy. But such findings as have been presented above identify a variety of factors tending to limit the returns that are expected to motivate industrial managements to make the large investments and to assume the heavy risks involved in major research programs and technological innovations. Accordingly, these results may also warrant consideration in the course of any review of the adequacy of public policies concerned with encouraging further technological progress in particular sectors of industry as well as in the economy as a whole.

6.8. PRODUCTIVITY AND TECHNOLOGY IMPROVEMENT EFFORTS: DETERRENTS AND POTENTIAL REMEDIAL MEASURES

As was noted early in this discussion, the most important sources of improvements in industrial productivity and technology are management decisions. These are determined by the expected relative profitability of alternative resource commitments compared to the magnitude of the investments, risks, and other burdens involved; and improvements in productivity and technology usually represent only a small sector of the array of alternatives to be considered. Hence, reduced rates of progress in respect to productivity levels and technological advances in wide sectors of industry are probably attributable in large measure to managerial perceptions that the attractiveness of prospective returns from such undertakings has declined relative to other resource commitments.

In order to consider means of encouraging managerial decisions that seek advances in productivity and technology, attention will be turned first to the basic options available to them in promoting such gains, then to the dominant factors influencing their choices, and finally to the means whereby trade unions and the government could encourage greater commitments to such improvements.

6.8.1. Practical Decision Options

Not all of the eight factors that have been identified as major sources of changes in industrial productivity levels are primarily controlled by management decisions. Changes in capacity utilization, in product-mix, and in the supply and quality of available labor and materials tend to be dominated by changes in market conditions—and to dominate short-term changes in productivity relationships in most industries. Thus, as was indicated earlier, because of the limited downward flexibility of labor and capital, recurrent increases in capacity utilization tend to be accompanied by increases in output per man-hour and in output relative to net fixed investment up to the point where further increases require resorting to less efficient facilities, employing less efficient labor and lower quality materials, and exceeding optimal production schedules. Over the longer run, the most influential of these external pressures on productivity levels, aside from broad economic conditions, is likely to be changes in the availability and quality of materials and fuels—declines tending partially or wholly to offset contributions toward higher productivity from other sources.

Among the decisions affecting productivity levels controlled by management, two tend to be dominated by nontechnological considerations: labor relations and the span of operations. The latter takes the form of very infrequent decisions involving large long-term investments with attendant risks—decisions that are heavily influenced by procurement and marketing considerations—with resulting changes in productivity levels (whether increases or decreases) given lesser weight. On the other hand, labor-relations decisions rank among the most important influences on productivity levels. Their primary focus in the short run is obviously to provide effective incentives for maximum sustainable efforts to increase the volume and improve the quality of production. Toward that end, there have been widespread management agreements to raise average wage rates in proportion to increases in physical output per man-hour, often supplemented by increasing allowances to cover changes in the cost of living, time off for illness and vacations, contributions to unemployment and pension benefits, and various forms of insurance. The primary additional focus of industrial relations over the longer run is increasingly being recognized by management as gaining unrestricted acceptance of technological innovations. Although such management commitments have involved very substantial costs, it is not at all clear that they have intensified labor's efforts to increase production and quality. Even more serious is currently increasing evidence of resistance to technological innovations that threaten existing employment and skill levels. Needless to say, such rising costs and restricted benefits represent one of the important elements in managerial evaluations of the attractiveness of prospective investments in seeking further improvements in productivity levels and technology.

Managerial decisions offering reasonably continuous short-term gains in productivity levels through technological developments center around programs seeking incremental improvements in the utilization of materials and energy, in the efficiency of existing facilities and equipment, in the integration of production operations, and in the design of products, although the latter may also be motivated by efforts to increase their attractiveness to buyers even at the expense of reducing productivity levels. Such programs usually entail relatively modest financial commitments combined with small risks. But they are also likely to yield only small gains in productivity and even smaller market rewards, in view of the likelihood of similar efforts by competitors.

Only three major areas of managerial decisions affecting productivity and technology remain: modernizing existing plants through the purchase of new equipment and facilities embodying technological improvements; building new plants harnessing increased scale economies as well as technological advances; and establishing long-term research and development programs seeking major advances in products, in processes, and in production facilities and equipment. Modernization programs would involve moderate investments as compared to those required by new plants, would entail small technological risks, and would offer the moderate rewards of catching up with some hitherto superior competitors. Building new plants would obviously require larger and longer-term investments and would involve increased market risks and technological risks as well (depending on the extent of the new technological and scale advances to be embodied). If successful, however, it would also be expected to offer higher rates of return after completion and the attainment of high levels of utilization.

In short, the last three constitute the most important sources of substantial advances in productivity levels and technology controlled by management decisions. And the increasing potential magnitudes of their respective contributions tend to be paralleled by increases in the magnitude, duration, and riskiness of the financial commitments required.

6.8.2. Disparities in Decision-Making Frameworks

It is important to recognize that firms and industries may differ widely not only in their evaluations of the relative profitability of major improvements in productivity levels as compared to other managerial efforts, but also in their evaluations of different kinds of productivity and technological advances. For example, in consumer goods industries accustomed to very modest rates of technological change and whose markets are strongly responsive to product differentiation and to innovations in sales and distribution efforts, managements are likely to restrict technological improvement efforts to seeking evolutionary improvements in product design and in production methods. Such tendencies tend to be reinforced by the limited capacity of most buyers to evaluate technical improvements, thus permitting the potential penalties of lagging behind competitors to be moderated through the intensification of marketing efforts and the introduction of lesser, but distracting, improvements.

In industries with slowly changing technologies producing largely undifferentiated products and hence operating in markets that are responsive to price differentials among competitors, reductions in production costs are likely to be a major target of management. Special efforts might accordingly be expected to increase productivity levels in the short run through incremental improvements in the efficiency of existing facilities and equipment as well as in the integration of operations. Significant gains might also be expected from modernization. But long-term commitments to developing scale economies and basic process improvements might well be limited unless trends in demand suggested a need in the not too distant future for new plants with such advanced capabilities.

In industries subject to rapid technological advances and selling to technologically sophisticated buyers, however, managements have no alternatives to making heavy commitments to the development of major product innovations. Major production innovations may also be important, of course, but their benefits might fade quickly with new product developments.[18]

In addition to such extreme cases, firms and industries may obviously differ in respect to the relative urgency of expanding output, increasing product quality, and adjusting to lower quality materials or restrictions on energy consumption, as opposed to increasing productivity levels and reducing production costs.[19] Moreover, even within a given industry, firms may differ in their readiness to rely on gaining significant cost advantages through increases in productivity as opposed to concentrating on other means of increasing profitability, including marketing innovations, changes in pricing strategies, shifts in financing, and so forth. Such differences may reflect the past expertise of top management, past experience with the various alternatives, or emulation of the tactics of leading competitors.[20]

Considerations such as the foregoing may help to explain why the relative emphasis on advancing productivity levels and technology has differed among industries and will continue to do so. And they may also help to explain why the relative emphasis on such gains tends to fluctuate over time among firms in the same industry. But they do not explain evidence of a seemingly widespread tendency toward a decreasing rate of progress in industrial productivity levels in the United States over a period of years.

6.8.3. Decision Criteria and
Deterrents to Productivity Increases

In attempting to identify the factors that seem to have contributed to the general slowing down of such progress, attention will be given first to the determinants of relevant decisions in individual firms and then to factors tending to discourage commitments seeking to improve productivity and technological capabilities in industries at large.

Managerial Objectives. Presumably most managements seek to allocate available resources so as to promote attainment of the firm's objectives, among which the maintenance or improvement of profitability is usually given the heaviest weight. From the standpoint of the latter, alternatives are widely evaluated by comparing expected contributions to net profits, through increased margins between revenues and costs, with associated investment requirements, with future yields discounted.[21]

Increases in revenues may be achieved by various combinations of their four determinants: increasing productive capacity; easing output restrictions resulting from shortages of needed materials, energy, or labor; reducing product prices enough to stimulate offsetting increases in sales; and increasing the attractiveness of products through improvements in design and quality. And reductions in cost may obviously be achieved by decreasing the volume of inputs per unit of output, by shifting to lower-priced inputs, or by appropriate substitutions of some inputs for others.

Small improvements in both sets of determinants are attainable through relatively low-cost and low-risk allocations to product modification, materials engineering, and production engineering. But such efforts are likely to yield diminishing improvements in productivity and even fewer benefits in cost reductions within given plants using established facilities and equipment. Physical productivity gains tend to decline as past rates of idleness and wastage are progressively reduced, as fuller use of equipment capabilities is achieved, and as shortcomings of coordination and control are minimized. Moreover, resulting cost savings are likely to fall short of paralleling some productivity gains because of factor price increases. Thus, increases in output per man-hour tend to engender largely or wholly offsetting increases in hourly wage rates to yield little if any reduction in unit wage costs, and the tightening of specifications for materials in order to reduce the quantity required per unit of output often involves at least partially offsetting increases in price. Conversely, shifts to cheaper materials often result in increasing the volume of such inputs per unit of output. Incidentally, this latter expedient may also undermine product quality, with possibly unfavorable repercussions on sales volume and prices.

But larger gains in revenues and cost savings require more basic advances in product development, production technologies, and operating facilities and equipment, and also their utilization through the modernization of existing plants and the construction of new plants embodying advances in scale as well as technology. As was noted earlier, however, these tend to require longer-term financial commitments and to involve larger technological and market risks. Moreover, although the projects that prove successful are likely to yield more generous rewards, these tend to become available only after extended periods of waiting, thus shrinking the present value of such eventual gains.

It is important to recall at this point that the higher past trends in productivity resulted from adding the contributions of these major advances to those of smaller improvements. Between these two sources of further gains, it is probable that there has been less of a decline in the continuity of efforts to achieve such smaller gains than in those seeking more substantial advances. It is unlikely, therefore, that past rates of progress in the productivity and technological capabilities of U.S. industries can be regained, much less surpassed, unless the sources of major advances are reinvigorated.

Some Widespread Deterrents.   One of the most powerful deterrents to projects seeking major advances in productivity and technology is the prevailing emphasis on short-term profitability combined with the high costs and risks of long-term research and the construction of large innovative production facilities. Increasing weight has been given to short-term profitability for a variety of reasons. One of these has been the growing use of formal capital-budgeting methods that provide for the explicit discounting of future returns—and that have tended to shorten investment horizons further in recent years as discount rates have risen.[22] A second reason has been the increasing role in stock ownership and trading of institutions under great pressure to maximize short-term returns and with little basis in terms of personal involvement for long-term commitments to any given firm, as a result of which reductions in profitability tend to engender prompt stock-price penalties and attendant pressures on management. A third reason has been increasing uncertainty about longer-term economic prospects in a wide array of industries, often less than fully reflected in quantitative discount rates.

Such pressures have tended to encourage concentration on projects that can be completed more quickly and that involve relatively smaller financial commitment, rather than facing the prospect of declining profitability over an extended period as increasing resources are absorbed into long-term undertakings that yield no additional revenues until they come to fruition. In respect to research, this has tended to favor pursuing immediately applicable objectives rather than more basic ones, emphasizing modest product improvements rather than achieving major advances in key processes, and catching up with actual or threatened achievements by others rather than attempting adventuresome pioneering.[23] In respect to the adoption of innovations developed by others, an emphasis on short-term profitability tends to favor waiting until both technological and market risks seem to have been substantially reduced. As for building large new plants embodying innovative technologies, such pressures make it more difficult to obtain needed financing if substantial revenues are not likely to be forthcoming within three to four years, especially in industries subject to substantial fluctuations in capacity utilization.

A second widespread deterrent to commitments to improving industrial productivity and technology has been the diminishing prospective economic benefits even from successful advances in production technologies and facilities. Because unit wage cost differences have been a significant source of competitive advantages in many industries, prospective gains in this area have been a major stimulus to technological development efforts in the past. Such undertakings are being discouraged, however, by increasing trade union pressures in two directions: to resist technically feasible reductions in employment levels, and to raise hourly wage rates in proportion to any permitted decreases in man-hour per unit of output. Expected unit wage cost benefits tend thereby to be largely or wholly eliminated, even though man-hour inputs are most often being decreased not through intensified production efforts by labor, but rather by substituting capital for labor through technological advances involving new processes, larger-scale facilities, and increased automation. Under such conditions, the accompanying increases in fixed capital charges tend to result in raising rather than lowering average total costs per unit of output, especially in industries subject to substantial fluctuations in output.[24] It should be recognized, however, that the potential benefits of major technological innovations in reducing unit labor costs may be substantially more promising if the innovations are embodied in new plants in new locations instead of being subject to attempts to retrofit them into existing plants with highly developed resistances in the form of established work rules, skill classifications, and incentive pay arrangements.

The possibility of increasing the productivity of capital has been another source of stimulus to projects seeking to improve processing technologies and to achieve greater economies of scale. Substantial advances have been achieved on both fronts in a wide range of industries, but expected benefits have fallen significantly short of expectations because of the long-established rising trend in capital goods prices and construction costs. As for decreasing material and energy requirements per unit of output, technological advances have been largely offset by the decreasing quality and rising price of most and by the increasing investments required to utilize the technological advances.

The repeated references above to increasing capital requirements merely reflect the widespread tendency in virtually all industries toward the increasing dominance of capacity levels and productive efficiency by the modernity and scale of facilities and equipment. There are few production industries except for handicraft operations in which labor-dominance continues, and equally few in which materials are dominant. Both of these have tended to move at first toward "joint-dominance," as in automobile assembly plants, machine tool factories, and metal smelters, but with virtually all further changes tending to increase the role of facilities, equipment, instrumentation, and computerized controls. Accordingly, this must be a primary focus of efforts to improve industrial productivity and technology.

One more factor tending to reduce the potential economic benefits of efforts to develop technological advances is the government's heavy participation in profits when such efforts are successful, combined with its withdrawal from sharing the losses likely to result from many (and perhaps most) efforts to advance major industrial technologies significantly.

A third important deterrent to efforts to advance industrial productivity and technology derives from various government regulatory activities. Few government regulatory activities are universally regarded as devoid of benefits. Their consideration here will be limited, however, to their possible bearing on the apparent decline in industrial programs to develop and to apply major advances in productivity and technology.

Environmental pollution controls represent one of the important sources of such deterrents. Such negative pressures do not derive from the principle of reducing pollution, but rather from the level of the standards set, the speed of required progress, and the methods of implementation. It is obvious that pollution controls will divert some investment and technical manpower programs to increase productivity and the effectiveness of production technology. The relevant question concerns how much of such diversions is desirable from the standpoint of the national welfare, considering the latter to include the maintenance and improvement of industrial competitiveness. Clearly, the higher the standards set and the shorter the period allowed to achieve compliance, the greater such diversions are likely to be, with reduced inputs left to improve productivity and technology. Moreover, the less integrated the demands for controlling air and water pollution as well as related health and safety standards, the more wasteful are industry's responses to such separate demands likely to be.

Another deterrent derived from pollution controls is the long drawn-out and costly process of analyzing and evaluating the prospective environmental impact of new plants. Delays of one or two years, and even longer in some cases, combined with additional outlays for special studies unrelated to plant requirements, may represent formidable additions to the burdens to be overcome before deciding to go ahead and thus may further reduce the likelihood of such a decision or at least delay it in favor of other options thereby rendered relatively more attractive.

One of the important sources of improved technological capabilities in recent years has been increasing the scale of operating units, whether ships, power plants, cement mills, petroleum refineries, pulp plants, or steel mills. Effective development and utilization of such facilities, however, have tended to encourage increases in the size of the firms operating such units and hence increases in the dominance of many industries by a relatively small number of firms. In other countries, the harnessing of these potential increases in efficiency and competitive advantages has been actively supported by government. In the United States, however, our official commitment to maintaining effective competition in industries has been interpreted as requiring resistance to whatever may be considered "excessive" concentration at different periods by different officials. This has tended to discourage efforts to realize the full potentials of scale increases, lest successes reduce the number of competitors and thus invite government threats or even penalties.

Finally, it should be noted that the government's frequent and increasingly widespread, though mostly unofficial, pressures against price increases has introduced an additional source of uncertainty in evaluations of the prospective profitability of developing new technologies or building large new plants in industries facing prospective capacity shortages. Such threats to the likelihood that higher prices will be available to those prepared to make investments to help cope with expected shortages can only serve as additional discouragements.

A fourth deterrent applicable to an increasing array of industries derives from uncertainty about the willingness of the U.S. government to prevent unfair competition in domestic markets from imports subsidized by foreign governments. As the largest and most affluent market in the world, the United States is the prime target of export drives from developing countries, as well as from Western Europe and Japan. Many of these governments regard the expansion of such exports as less burdensome, even if based on subsidies and pricing below cost, than increases in unemployment payments and accompanying increases in political opposition.[25] Moreover, not many of our industries could survive determined government-supported invasions of our markets, as indicated most recently by the extraordinary terms offered to Eastern Airlines to purchase the European Airbus. Hence, domestic producers are deterred by the likelihood that any cost reductions that might be obtained through technological development programs would be offset by import price adjustments supported by foreign governments committed to maintaining or expanding their exports, regardless of whether their producers fall behind technologically or sell below cost.[26] But such deterrence also tends to ensure progressive deterioration of the competitive position of domestic producers relying on increasingly aging technology and facilities (Gold and Boylan, 1975).

6.8.4. Potential Remedial Measures

What can be done to increase the rate of advances in industrial productivity and technology in the United States? To intensify managerial efforts toward that end, it is obviously necessary to increase the expected profitability of doing so as compared with alternative means of improving the firm's performance. The evaluation of such relative rewards is based on an array of components representing internal staff evaluations, expected trade union reactions, and, perhaps most important of all, the estimated effects of a variety of government policies. More favorable contributions may be necessary from each in order to effect a substantial acceleration of progress in the technological capabilities of wide sectors of domestic industry.

Intrafirm Measures.   The single most important stimulus to productivity levels and technological progress in a firm is the degree and continuity of top management's commitment to such objectives. From this commitment derive implementing policies, which are reflected by budget allocations, performance targets, and criteria for determining rewards.

To be effective, resulting task assignments and evaluations must be discriminating. Those concerned with improving physical productivity levels should be given targets in such terms and should have their results appraised in such terms, instead of being evaluated solely in terms of cost effects, which include the impact of factor price changes that are beyond their control and that are in any event the responsibility of different specialists. The offsetting effects on costs of inflationary factor prices in recent years have tended to minimize recognition of labor and materials productivity achievements and thereby to reduce rewards and attendant incentives for such efforts.[27]

Japanese experience suggests that significant benefits can be achieved through increasing the throughput capacity of most existing facilities and equipment. They commonly use a higher ratio of engineers to labor and subject engineers to continuous aggressive pressure to keep increasing the capacity and reducing the energy and other input requirements of available facilities by 3 to 5 percent each year, through intensive efforts to modify tooling, accessories, operating methods, and even equipment components that limit performance.[28] My field studies suggest that such pressures are much less continuous and intensive in U.S. industries, partly because extended periods of capacity underutilization have blunted managerial interest in increasing capacity further. But the easing of such pressures cannot but undermine the drive of engineers to keep surpassing past performance. It is also worth noting that cumulative increases in the capacity of existing partially depreciated facilities can result in major savings of investment relative to the sharply inflated costs of new additions to capacity.

The need to deepen top management commitments to improving productivity and technology is also suggested by evidence of surprising tolerance for wide differences in such performance among the plants of multiplant firms. Seemingly logical reasons are often accepted without penetrating tests, and persistent differences come to be accepted as somehow unchangeable, as indeed they tend to become when prevailing performance levels have long been accepted by the plant management, their technical personnel, and the labor force. Only powerful new pressures from top management implemented by close monitoring of results, and by the reflection of results in promotions and salaries, are likely to overcome such inertias.

Equally important is the need for management to develop more effective support from its work force for continuing improvements in productivity and technology. Headway has been made in many industries over the years through incentive payments, bonuses for suggestions to increase effectiveness, and even through threats of layoffs. But the tendency for labor to identify with management's need for increased productive efficiency is not widespread in U.S. industries. Even more serious is the widespread belief among the labor force that their interests conflict with those of management: that management seeks to reduce employment, decrease skills, hold down wage rates, and minimize fringe benefits. There is, of course, ample basis for such adversary viewpoints. Nevertheless, the challenge remains—and it is one of the most serious regarding the survival of our present form of economy—to increase *evidences* of management's concern to minimize the hardship of its work force and to show how improvements in productivity and technology can contribute heavily to such ends. It should be emphasized, however, that progress in this direction is more likely to be achieved (1) plant by plant and firm by firm rather than through general industrywide and national drives, and (2) through specific actions in the form of commitments and safeguards rather than through exhortations.

Trade Union Measures. Because democratic trade unions must be responsive to their membership, it is especially difficult for their officials, who face periodic reelections, to develop any cooperative relationships with management without being challenged by "rank-and-file" extremists. It seems reasonably clear that minimizing long-run reductions in employment levels and maximizing long-run wage rates and fringe benefits in industries subject to competition from imports or substitute products require continuing advances in productivity and technology. But this tends to be much less self-evident in the short run, and short-run considerations commonly overshadow long-term implications in the course of periodic elections.

As a result, trade union managements face as challenging a problem as company executives. As was suggested above, this will require courageous efforts to explore with management how improvements in productivity and technology can be harnessed so as to save jobs and improve earnings, while also minimizing accompanying hardships. Progress is more likely to take the form of a succession of limited agreements, of course, rather than an all-embracing program. But each advance may be used both to join with management in seeking any governmental help that may be needed and to demonstrate to the majority of union members the superiority of such policies as compared with unrestrained opposition to all productivity and technological improvements. It is to be hoped that the higher education levels and generally improved living standards of the present labor force have improved the possibilities of gaining a sympathetic response to such constructive efforts.

However, trade unions, too, have to supplement agreements in principle with supporting actions. Thus, for example, there are current instances of national trade unions avowing acceptance of all technological innovations, while some of their local branches clearly restrict the implementation of available advances. Blame for acquiescence in such resistance must be shared, of course, by local managements fearful of the effects of labor resistance on their plant's performance. But cooperation between corporate managements and trade union officials is not likely to advance very far if it cannot cope with such early tests.

Governmental Measures.   If government leaders truly consider it important in the national interest to induce greater efforts to improve industrial productivity and technology, consideration should be given to easing or eliminating some of the deterrents rooted in current government policies—and perhaps to adding some incentives as well. But the effectiveness of such special measures will depend in large measure on the development and maintenance of more promising long-run prospects for the national economy. Increasing confidence in continuing economic growth, combined with receding threats of mounting inflation—with resulting expectations of expanding markets and attractive profits—would help to generate a momentum of willingness to undertake riskier, longer-term commitments, which it would be difficult to duplicate under conditions of great economic uncertainty despite special governmental measures. In the absence of discouraging economic prospects, however, special measures may help to engender quite substantial gains.

One group of corrective measures might be directed toward increasing the rewards from undertakings offering only long-delayed benefits and also reducing their costs and risks. For example, substantially more favorable tax treatment of the capital gains or delayed profits derived from long-term projects that improve productivity and technology would help to offset the pressures of high discount rates against such undertakings.[29] Additional incentives would be provided by permitting accelerated depreciation or, even better, by permitting depreciation charges to begin with the onset of construction, thus reducing the average net investment embodied in capital projects providing needed improvements in productivity and technology but requiring long construction periods.[30] To reduce the high risks of programs seeking to develop substantial advances in basic technologies, consideration should be given to governmental incentives beyond merely permitting firms to write off attendant losses. Perhaps heavy governmental sharing in any resulting profits should be balanced by some form of sharing in losses. Especially urgent but risky projects might be encouraged by cost-sharing government grants, either to individual firms or to joint projects of several companies.

Still another potentially powerful source of stimulus would be the development of an array of joint industry-government–financed research centers in association with major universities that would conduct continuing programs of basic research seeking to strengthen the scientific foundations of applied technology for each of a number of major industries. Such an innovation would represent a belated extension to industry of the government's enormous long-term contributions to developing the technological capabilities of American agriculture through the establishment of numerous research centers; such centers would also help to offset the special advantages of widespread governmental support for industrial research in other industrial nations.

Most of these measures would tend to increase the impetus to improvements in productivity and technology, thereby increasing the competitive position of domestic industries and attendant employment and income levels. While the suggested adjustments in tax policies would certainly alter the time pattern of tax receipts from the projects to be encouraged, it is not at all clear that they would reduce such receipts over the life of these undertakings, the reverse being far more likely in view of resulting growth and profitability. At any rate, standing pat with existing tax provisions will surely tend to reinforce recent tendencies to slow the rate of improvements in industrial productivity and technology.

It would obviously be undesirable for the government to become regularly involved in management-union negotiations about the absorption of improvements in productivity and technology. But consideration might well be given to developing means of providing three kinds of contributions to the easing of related problems. One of these might involve helping to reduce prospective attacks on management and union officials for introducing major technological innovations by offering to prepare, in response to joint requests, objective and expert evaluations of the prospective effects on competitiveness and employment of rejecting such available advances. Another might help to ease labor resistance to employment-threatening innovations by making available the same benefits of hardship payments and subsidized training opportunities now provided to the victims of import-induced unemployment. A third form of contribution might result from establishing an "early warning center" to identify newly diffusing technologies likely to engender labor problems and unemployment, which could serve as a basis for alerting company and trade union specialists, as well as government agencies, likely to be involved in dealing with such difficulties.

The government is obviously concerned with promoting economic opportunities and standards of living, as well as with minimizing the social costs of such advances. Hence, it must develop more effective means of preventing the dispersion of responsibilities in these two areas among agencies that have a monopolizing concern with any one of these objectives and that ignore or even take a hostile position relative to the concomitant effects of concern to others. The above examples of concern with encouraging improvements in productivity and technology thus may well encounter opposition from agencies concerned only with imminent tax receipts or agencies concerned solely with reducing unemployment; antagonisms may also be generated by agencies committed to minimizing pollution, helping to preserve small business, or seeking to minimize obstacles to imports.

In the case of pollution controls, needed governmental contributions center around moderating (not minimizing) the diversion of scarce capital and technical personnel from projects yielding significant advances in productivity and production processes. This would involve adjusting the required rate of reductions in pollution to what could be accomplished with reasonable allocations of such resources. It would also involve restricting required pollution control investments to equipment demonstrably capable of meeting planned standards for an extended period of time, instead of risking repeated replacements. In addition, it would be helpful to develop integrated air and water pollution standards that resolve any state and federal differences as the basis for asking plants to develop integrated programs assuring increasing conformance to such standards. Finally, it is becoming increasingly essential for the government to develop more expeditious procedures for evaluating and making decisions about the prospective environmental impacts of new plants.

To prevent the progressive undermining of a considerable array of private industries in this country by uneconomically priced or otherwise government-supported imports would seem to require that the U.S. government make a determined effort to restore fair competition in our markets and also to secure access for our exports to foreign markets on fully comparable terms. Both long-run and immediate measures would be essential to assure American producers against a resurgence of such practices whenever overseas pressures are intensified. Such efforts need not, however, discriminate against imports on the basis of lower wage rates abroad. Indeed, one of the objectives of improving domestic productivity and technology is to permit our labor force to compete with such imports by raising productivity levels sufficiently to justify higher wage rates.

Another sector of government deterrents to advances in productivity and technology could be eased by revising antitrust policies so as to encourage increases in scale and advances in technology that offer significant gains in productive efficiency, even if they lead to greater concentration, provided that effective competition is maintained. This might require only that persuasive evidence be required to prove claims of reduced competition instead of regarding mere increases in concentration as inherent proof of such claims.

There are many urgent reasons, of course, for intensifying efforts to accelerate improvements in industrial productivity and technology. Recent public awareness has been triggered primarily by the threats to employment of increasing imports in a variety of industries. But other needs are both more important and more pervasive. Improvements in productivity and technology may well prove to be the soundest and most fruitful means of easing inflationary pressures; increasing the effective utilization of natural resources; minimizing industrial health, safety, and pollution hazards; and also raising national standards of living. Such potential benefits are obviously accompanied by substantial costs, risks, and even some undesirable effects. But that is all the more reason for attempts such as this to examine the larger framework of considerations bearing on the development of objectives and policies seeking to optimize potential results.

This discussion suggests that major improvements will require new policies, rather than the mere reiteration of past exhortations, on the part of industrial managements as well as trade unions and the government. Moreover, analysis of past experience suggests that substantial commitments will be necessary over extended periods of time, combined with continuing evaluations of progress and shortcomings, if significant advances are to be achieved over the next five years.

NOTES

1. Detailed empirical evidence in support of the judgments presented in the following analysis is not included in the interest of brevity, but their sources are cited, of course.
2. For further discussion, see Gold, 1955, pp. 6–12.
3. For an early discussion of this problem, see Gold, 1964, p. 126. For a reference to later publications dealing with this problem, see Nelson, Peck, and Kalachek, 1967, pp. 32–33.
4. For further discussion, see Gold, 1977c, Chapters 2, 3, 7, and 8.
5. For more detailed discussions, see Gold, 1977a, and Gold, 1971, pp. 44–48.
6. For an empirical exploration of such wider ramifications, see Nelson, 1962.
7. For a discussion of the limitations of input-output analysis in this connection, see Erdilek, 1977, and Gold, 1977a.
8. For a detailed discussion of each of these sources of changes in productivity relationships as well as their effects, see Gold, 1955, pp. 107–66, 202–14.
9. The effect of such other considerations on the diffusion rates of productivity-improving innovations is discussed in Gold, Peirce, and Rosegger, 1970, and their effects on scale decisions are considered in Gold, 1974.
10. For an early detailed analysis, see Gold, 1971, pp. 59–66; for later data, see Gold, 1975b, p. 15.
11. Incidentally, when the productivity of capital (defined as the ratio of productive investment to net fixed investment) is increased through the reduction in net investment by depreciation allowances, there is a similar absence of practical options because this productivity gain can seldom be transformed into an equivalent gain in capacity combined with no change in the level of fixed investment.
12. For a more detailed discussion, see Gold, 1955, pp. 182–88.
13. This concept is fundamentally different from the traditional meaning of *capital-intensive*. The latter is commonly applied to plants and firms with a relatively high ratio of capital costs to total costs, as in the case of electricity-generating plants where such ratios may approximate 40 percent or more. But *capital-intensive* is also often mistakenly applied to operations characterized by large amounts of fixed investment and capital facilities, although these need not result in large ratios of capital costs to total costs. For example, this term is frequently applied to the steel industry because of its enormous capital requirements, although total depreciation and interest charges for major steel companies usually average 10 percent or less of total costs. In contrast, our use of the term *capital-dominated* refers instead to the extent to which productive capacity can be altered by changes in the capital facilities as compared to the effect on capacity of changes in labor or material inputs. For a more detailed discussion, see Gold, 1955, pp. 188–96, 215–30.
14. For a detailed discussion, see Gold, 1955, pp. 188–95.
15. One should not concentrate, as Salter (1966) did, solely on technological responses to change in factor prices without also going on to consider the subsequent repercussions on factor prices. For further discussion and related empirical findings, see Gold, 1971, pp. 193–97.
16. For a further discussion of the vulnerability of these hypotheses, see Gold, 1976, pp. 19–26.

17. For further discussion, see Gold, 1976.
18. For further discussion, see Gold, 1975*a*, pp. 26–27.
19. For fuller discussion, see Gold, Peirce, and Rosegger, 1970, pp. 233–35.
20. For fuller discussion, see Gold, 1969, pp. 397–407.
21. For further discussion of the components of such models and attendant problems of evaluation, see Gold, 1977*b*.
22. For example, a discount rate of even 15 percent would reduce the present value of future returns by more than 25 percent if available after two years and by nearly 50 percent if available after four years. For further discussion, see Gold and Boylan, 1975.
23. President Carter was recently quoted as expressing concern about the fact that "in recent years, industry has concentrated more and more on low risk, short term projects directed at improving existing products." He said an emphasis on longer-term projects is "closely related" to economic productivity and U.S. competitiveness in world markets (*Wall Street Journal, May 12, 1978*).
24. For detailed empirical findings over an extended period in the steel industry, see Gold, 1976.
25. For example, in reporting on the current status of international trade negotiations, *Business Week* (June 12, 1978, p. 66) noted that "most serious obstacles to agreement are government subsidies to industry and barriers to agricultural trade. European governments regard it as their sovereign right to subsidize industries for purposes such as maintaining employment, even if the result is to distort normal trading patterns." This is especially relevant to the U.S. steel industry because the largest recent surge in imports came from European producers despite the fact that their production costs are not lower than here.
26. "British steel lost $820 Million last year on 13.4 Million metric tons. Third successive year of substantial losses" (*New York Times,* July 5, 1978). "Italian producers, mainly government-owned, have dropped $850 Million since 1975; state-owned British Steel Corp., the European Community's biggest producer, has lost $1.44 Billion and stands to pass the $2 Billion loss mark this year. Desperate French steelmakers have asked for a moratorium on long-term debt. Even Germany's relatively new, integrated mills are in their fourth year of losses in a row" (*Business Week,* July 17, 1978 p. 40).
27. For example, in evaluating proposed capital projects, some firms refuse to permit the inclusion of expected labor-cost savings on the grounds that such expectations have usually been unfulfilled.
28. For more detailed discussion, see Gold, 1978*b*.
29. This might be regarded as a form of "reverse discount incentive" to encourage needed longer-term undertakings.
30. For example, in the case of projects requiring six to ten years of construction period (electric power plants, steel mills, etc.), such depreciation practices might reduce average net investment by one-third to one-half.

REFERENCES

Baier, K., and N. Rescher, eds., 1969, *Values and the Future,* New York, Free Press (paperback edition, 1971).

De Bandt, J., ed., 1978, *Le capital dans la fonction de production,* Paris: Centre National de la Recherche Scientifique.

Eilon S., B. Gold, and J. Soesan, 1976a, *Applied Productivity Analysis for Industry,* Oxford: Pergamon Press.

———, 1976b, "Production Changes in a Chemical Plant," *Omega,* June.

Erdilek, A., 1977, "Productivity, Technological Change and Input-Output Analysis," in Gold (1977c).

Fabricant, S., 1939, *The Output of Manufacturing Industries, 1899–1937,* New York: National Bureau of Economic Research.

Gold, B., 1978a, "On the Role of Capital in Production: A Revision of Some Basic Concepts," in De Bandt (1978).

———, 1978b, "Steel Technology and Costs in the U.S. and Japan," *Iron and Steel Engineer,* April.

———, 1977a, "Research, Technological Change and Economic Analysis," *Quarterly Review of Economics and Business,* Spring.

———, 1977b, "On the Shaky Foundations of Capital Budgeting," *California Management Review,* Winter.

———, ed., 1977c, *Research, Technological Change, and Economic Analysis,* Lexington, Mass.: Lexington Books.

———, 1976, "Tracing Gaps between Expectations and Results of Technological Innovations: The Case of Iron and Steel," *Journal of Industrial Economics,* September.

———, 1975a, "Alternative Strategies for Advancing a Company's Technology," *Research Management,* July.

———, ed., 1975b, *Technological Change: Economics, Management and Environment,* Oxford: Pergamon Press.

———, 1974, "Evaluating Scale Economies: The Case of Japanese Blast Furnaces," *Journal of Industrial Economics,* September.

———, 1971, *Explorations in Managerial Economics,* London: Macmillan; New York: Basic Books.

———, 1969, "The Decision Framework for Major Technological Innovations," in Baier and Rescher (1969).

———, 1964, "Economic Effects of Technological Innovations," *Management Science,* September.

———, 1955, *Foundations of Productivity Analysis,* Pittsburgh: University of Pittsburgh Press.

Gold, B., and M. G. Boylan, 1975, "Capital Budgeting, Industrial Capacity and Imports," *Quarterly Journal of Economics and Business,* Fall.

Gold, B., W. G. Peirce, and G. Rosegger, 1970, "Diffusion of Major Technological Innovations in U.S. Iron and Steel Manufacturing," *Journal of Industrial Economics,* July.

Hildred, W. M., J. D. Nadler, and L. A. Bengston, 1978, "Innovation Accounting and Productivity Data in Electronics Manufacturing Firms: Two Case Studies," Report to the National Science Foundation, Denver, January.

Kendrick, J. W., 1961, *Productivity Trends in the U.S.,* Princeton, N.J.: Princeton University Press.

Nelson, R. R., M. J. Peck, and E. D. Kalachek, 1967, *Technology, Economic Growth and Public Policy,* Washington, D.C.: Brookings.

Nelson, R. R., ed., 1962, *The Rate and Direction of Inventive Activity: Economic and Social Factors,* Princeton, N.J.: Princeton University Press.

Peirce, W. G., 1975, "The Effects of Technological Change: Exploring Successive Ripples," in Gold (1975*b*).

Salter, W. E. G., 1966, *Productivity and Technical Change,* Cambridge: Cambridge University Press.

Schmookler, J., 1952, "The Changing Efficiency of the American Economy," *Review of Economics and Statistics,* August.

Skeddle, R. W., 1977, "Empirical Perspectives on Major Capital Decisions," Ph.D. dissertation, Case Western Reserve University.

7 PRODUCTIVITY AND PRODUCTION MANAGEMENT

Martin K. Starr

7.1. INTRODUCTION

There has been a productivity problem in the United States for many years, but it had gone unnoticed until recently. It is reflected by a decreasing rate of growth of productivity, the importance of which was not recognized as quickly as its symptoms: inflation, unemployment, weak currency, and deficit trade balances. With near-zero productivity growth, the existence of a problem was generally acknowledged. Probing articles appeared in 1979 (McConnell, 1979; Malkiel, 1979b). The question being asked is, What causes the problem?

Many answers have been given to this question that are, at best, partly right. They involve worker alienation and changing composition of the work force, decreasing technological innovation, a shortage of fixed capital investment, and increasing regulatory inhibitors. None of these answers provides operational solutions to the problem. The future is not encouraging since economists continue to disagree about the causes of the slowdown in productivity growth.

Additional factors providing operational benefits that should be considered have not been. Production and operations managers are responsible for the actual productivity of the processes with which they deal on a day-to-day basis. They could improve productivity if they knew how to cope with the organizational constraints that seem to tie their hands. Financial planning that integrates marketing and distribution with production considerations is essential for a systems capability to maximize productivity.

We cannot expect economists to diagnose and prescribe on such a detailed level what work configurations would provide the best obtainable productivity. Furthermore, demand volumes reflect price elasticities that are tightly tied to costs that are highly elastic to supply volumes. Thus, when economists recommend steps to relieve capital shortages, they cannot prescribe how the new capital should be employed. And there is great reason to believe that under present circumstances, new capital will be employed in the least beneficial manner conceivable.

This is because production departments are not prepared to halt a fifteen-year trend of declining productivity growth that may well start eroding absolute productivity levels for the first time. Production managers do not understand that they can solve the productivity problem. Even so, every day the potential for increasing productivity through improved methods for scheduling, assigning, sequencing, inventorying, checking quality, and so forth, grows larger and cheaper to achieve with smaller, yet more powerful, computers. Even if they did know this, they would not have the clout to succeed. The production function has low organizational status. It began dropping at about the same time as the slowdown in productivity growth accelerated. Those who chose to stay in production may have less ambition, less desire to innovate, and less creativity than those who went elsewhere in the organization. In MBA programs all over the country, most students, including the best ones, concentrate in finance and marketing. Only a handful of students at Columbia's Graduate School of Business (many who come from abroad) choose the production and operations management concentration. But there are signs of improvement that, if encouraged by management, could result eventually in the return to rapid productivity growth in the United States.

Productivity is a complex performance variable comprised of many interacting components. It is responsive to specific controls that have been ignored in the literature dealing with causes of the productivity problem. This paper delineates some operational strategies that relate to improving the rate of growth of productivity in the United States.

7.2. PERCEPTION OF A PRODUCTIVITY PROBLEM

The symptoms of a problem are often treated long before the real problem is discovered. The treatment is often inadequate and frustrating because, at best, minor victories are replaced by worsening defeats. Thus, decreasing productivity growth fuels inflation. The dollar weakens against other currencies and serious trade deficits occur, especially when other countries maintain or increase their productivity growth. All of this is history.

For at least fifteen years, there has been a decline in the growth of productivity in the United States. However, only in the last several years has the measure approached zero growth. In fact, depending upon the inflation accounting that is used, it is conceivable that absolute productivity is decreasing. Such a state of affairs has called attention to a multifaceted problem that was going unrecognized by governmental officers and their economic advisers. Business executives did not recognize the seriousness of the situation, thinking that inflation was the cause of eroding productivity growth rather than the result of it. A paper by Starr (1973) illustrates this point. The paper, entitled "Productivity is the U.S.A.'s Problem," was rejected by two major business publications because the reviewers stated that since no productivity problem existed, the paper was obviously absurd. Finally, in 1973, the paper was published by the *California Management Review's* brave editor.

Part of the reason for not perceiving a productivity problem is that for years productivity was increasing, albeit at an ever slower rate. The measure—rate of change of productivity—is less visible and harder to track in managerial terms than is absolute productivity. Also, inflationary effects mask their cause and are most easily resolved by price increases, which maintain profitable income statements. At one time, an increase in a material's cost led to a managerial search for alternative production methods that would allow the price to be held, rather than passing the increase along to consumers. Such improved methods produced an increase in process productivity; but in the present economic environment, no pressure is felt for productivity improvement. The consumer and the producer expect regular price increases.

7.3. CAUSES OF PRODUCTIVITY PROBLEMS

Now that productivity problems have been recognized, a number of causes have been identified by economists (Malkiel, 1979*b*; McConnell, 1979). The list is extensive but can be characterized in four categories: decreasing worker contributions, increasing regulatory inhibition, decreasing technological innovation, and declining capital-labor ratio.

None of the factors contained within these four categories provides generally operational means for reversing the productivity decline. For example, with respect to *decreasing worker contributions,* the concept of alienation of young workers led one government official (without tongue in cheek) to state that the productivity problem will be solved by waiting for workers to age. In a deeper vein, the benefits of job enrichment are not well understood. Some workers seem to resent it. When it is beneficial, there is a job design problem dependent upon knowledge of the trade-offs between increased worker motivation and decreased productivity resulting from less specialization, about which not much is known. Other nonoperational factors are the changing composition of the work force, difficulties with unions, and the growth of the (inefficient) service sector's contribution to GNP.

Clearly, productivity growth has been *inhibited by governmental regulations.* But not much is known about the costs and benefits of such regulatory processes. Again, trade-off models must be built to describe the benefits and penalties accruing from different levels of control. For how much reduction of smoke-stack emission is the consumer willing to pay? What are the costs and benefits of health-hazard risk reduction resulting from the present auto-emission control program? Since risk is higher in 1980 than in 1985, should compensation be paid by the automobile manufacturers or the government to those afflicted by illness? Could anyone prove cause and effect? What costs and benefits are attributable to the Justice Department's regulation (and threat of regulation) of organizational size? What social costs and gains are involved in blocking the construction of new, highly productive refineries? Such interesting questions are baffling. Thus, the effects of regulation on productivity cannot be resolved in operational terms. We must seek other ways to deal with the productivity problem.

Whenever we read about forces that are decreasing productivity growth, we encounter the category of *diminishing technological innovation.* Unfortunately, there is little known about means to increase the societal advantage of government- or corporate-sponsored R&D. Abernathy (1979) states that high productivity decreases willingness to experiment with potential improvements. If so, something should be done to turn this around. Logically, new product failures must certainly contribute to decreases in productivity. The high rate of failures deserves regulatory attention, even though it may run counter to traditional views of "free competition." Operational steps for productivity improvement must deal with such contradictory statements as "High productivity stifles innovation" versus "Innovation is needed to reverse declines in productivity growth." There are also many unanswered questions. What tax rate on capital gains would promote innovation while fostering the public welfare? What is the net effect of decreasing capital shortages and increasing the capital-labor ratio, say, through tax incentives for technological innovation? This category raises more questions than it answers.

The most operational category of the economist's list of productivity factors is that of *increasing capital investment*. The United States is utilizing ancient equipment for production. In 1974, over 17 percent of U.S. business facilities were (at least) twenty years old. Technologically, over 14 percent were outmoded (Haynes, 1976, p. 34). Since that time, the situation has gotten progressively worse (see Kendrick, 1979, p. 5).

Of far greater importance, U.S. production methodologies are characteristic of a different era, being very successful twenty to thirty years ago and increasingly less so since that time. This is not well known because it relates to technical questions. Those capital investments that have been made have been "skewed toward equipment and relatively short-term projects and away from structures and relatively long-lived investments" (Malkiel, 1979*a*, p. 291). In other words, the investments maintain the old methods of doing work. Thus, productivity problems are not only related to a shortage of capital investments in productive capacity but also to the way that investment is used. Consequently, it would be helpful to answer two questions: First, do we know how to decrease the capital shortage? And second, if we can induce new capital investment, do we know how to use such capital? Economists are able to answer the first question. But they should do so bearing in mind the effect of a successful reply to the second question. If we don't know how to answer the second question, any answer to the first is not likely to matter.

7.4. FAILURE TO USE THE SYSTEMS APPROACH

There are detailed factors capable of providing productivity growth that have never been listed by the economists. This is because economists view the world in a macro way, whereas production and operations managers are responsible for the actual productivity of the processes with which they deal on a (micro-detailed) day-to-day basis. Production managers can translate the broad generalizations of the economists into specific terms that are bottom-line tests of their hypotheses.

As noted earlier, production managers could improve productivity if they knew how to cope with the organizational constraints that tie their hands. Financial planning generally ignores production possibilities while being receptive to market potentials. But production, marketing, distribution, and financial considerations must be treated together if maximum productivity is to be achieved. This is the systems approach.

Be our interests profits or societal benefits, we find that a systems viewpoint must prevail. The economists' factors are listed as if they were independent elements, each of which plays some part in creating or resolving the problem. The production manager, on the other hand, must perceive all of the elements as being totally interrelated. Of course, this includes motivating workers to contribute their best efforts and the hope that regulation will provide maximum trade-off benefits. It also reflects economically viable support of technological innovation (in the long term) and as much fixed capital investment as is needed to boost productivity (in the short run and the long run).

The systems approach for improving productivity growth is dependent upon a strong production department. But generally speaking, production departments are isolated, noncreative, and lack the drive to achieve greater organizational leverage. This state of affairs is well described by the Booz, Allen and Hamilton article "Merging Industrial Operations and Corporate Strategy" (1979). If production managers are to correct the productivity problem, they must first know how to redesign the production process to accomplish this result. Second, they must obtain organizational cooperation to support interfunctional planning (rather than the accustomed intrafunctional mode). At present, financial planning ignores the impact of production strategies on long-term, bottom-line performance while being receptive to relatively short-term market potentials. Such an attitude must surely take a gradual toll on industrywide productive performance.

Economists cannot diagnose and prescribe for systems-oriented production planning, with the need to specify on a detailed level what work configurations would provide the best obtainable productivity. Work configurations, as will be discussed in the next section, are not the servants of demand volumes since they can affect these; that is, demand volumes reflect price elasticities that are tightly tied to costs that are highly elastic to supply volumes. The Boston Consulting Group in hundreds of studies (1979) has found that increasing output volumes significantly decreases per unit costs of production. Accordingly, when economists recommend steps to relieve capital shortages, it is like prescribing medicine for treating an illness. The questions that must be answered are, What specific substances are to be taken? and How often? In this case, the recommendation that is needed is how the new capital should be employed. In other words, what work configurations will be most productive?

Since economists are not production managers, they expect that production and financial managers will work out the best way to utilize new capital for facility expansion. Unfortunately, there is reason to believe that under present conditions, new capital will be employed in almost the *least* beneficial manner conceivable.

This is because production managers are not prepared to do things differently. There is an ingrained inertia to keep the status quo. Plant design in the United States is, by world standards, committed to principles of production that are like investing in improvements of Model Ts to race Ferraris. As capital investment is obtained, it is used to increase the *efficiency* of the old (Model T) process. This makes it ever harder to replace the old-style process with a more *effective,* new type of system. Further, there are diminishing returns in pursuit of ever greater efficiencies from the old process.

Increased capital investment may temper, but it will not halt, a fifteen-year trend of declining productivity growth. Production managers do not even realize that they can solve their own productivity problems, let alone the nation's. Company after company across the United States could take advantage of the productivity potentials already modeled for them by Japan, West Germany, and other countries where restructuring of the production process has been going on for many years.

The keys to solution of the productivity problem are higher volume work configurations and greater reliance on methodological innovation. As previously noted, in the present organizational situation, even if production managers knew how to use these keys, they would not have the clout to succeed.

7.5. HIGHER VOLUME WORK CONFIGURATIONS

It is important to qualify the assumption that capital goods are "a carrier of new technology" (Kendrick, 1979, p. 4). The correctness of this assumption depends on how effectively the capital is used. To begin with, we must make every effort to bring about substantial changes in the way we do work.

What is needed is major capital investment planned to shift work configurations from relatively inefficient job shops to highly productive flow shops. Job shops cart work around in batches. Thus, finished goods enter inventory or are shipped from time to time as entire batches of work are completed. Flow-shop production lines perform repetitive activities in serialized form providing relatively continuous outputs.

Stated in terms of costs, flow shops have high fixed costs that permit low variable costs, whereas job shops have lower fixed costs and higher variable costs. The cost advantage of the flow shop is not realized until output volume reaches a high enough figure to justify its existence. Quality of the output of a flow shop can be higher than that of a job shop because of the greater investment in special-purpose equipment. Also, quality levels of the flow shop should be more consistent than those of the job shop.

The job shop can produce great output variety. While it is not generally known, so can the flow shop, although to achieve this requires a great deal of systems planning by production and market managers who conceive of the life cycles of the product line instead of using the buckshot approach of product-by-product planning. Also, the flow shop is often associated with the dehumanizing jobs and work conditions that Charlie Chaplin depicted in his movie decrying "mass production." With available technology employed in new ways, this stereotype can be forgotten, along with more recent memories of the General Motors strike at Lordstown, Ohio.

There are a lot of misconceptions about serialized production processes that must be cleared up, for the production manager as well as society at large. For example, if the production process is properly designed to achieve high productivity, then dull jobs assigned to workers should (and can) be eliminated. Machines can perform simple, repetitive functions better than humans can. As the work demands greater variability and decision-making capability, machines become less cost-effective. We have at our command in the 1980s an outstanding array of technological devices with incredible control capabilities residing in relatively inexpensive minicomputers. Only the barest fraction of the potential has been tapped. If we do this, the United States can construct the most productive processes in the world, bypassing those nations that are highly invested in 1970 technology. Trade deficits can become consistent surpluses.

7.6. ASSEMBLING HIGH DEMAND VOLUME

Another confusion is the belief that the flow shop cannot produce the kind of variety required by marketing. But this is not so. Using product-line planning and computer-controlled machinery, a variety of outputs can be obtained from the flow shop's high productivity process capabilities. In addition, the concept of modular production as described by Starr (1965) and further analyzed by Dogramaci (1979) has been used by a number of companies to increase the volume of demand for specific parts in which the company specializes. Low volume parts are subcontracted. This procedure was established long ago by Japanese trading companies that have governmental support to eliminate ineffective production configurations. Group technology is an additional concept that allows a company to specialize in families of parts, as described by Knayer (1970).

As previously noted (Boston Consulting Group, 1979), increases in supply volume are rewarded with decreasing costs that allow sales prices to be lowered, or quality to be improved, or both. Why should this decrease occur? First, increasing output rates are supported by more special-purpose equipment and require less human resources. When properly managed, increased revenues should result in a larger contribution that supports (in turn) the greater capitalization required for special-purpose equipment. Sec-

ond, larger output volumes permit greater quantity orders of vendor-sup-
plied materials that should result in improved discounts.

Imagine ten firms each producing ten items in a job-shop configuration,
as shown in Figure 7.1. Without sufficient volume, none of these companies
can be optimal producers—that is, have the lowest possible per unit costs.
Because of their batch-work configurations, all ten firms suffer substantial
defectives necessitating rework and disposal as scrap. Because of order
sizes, no inventory discounts are available. Further, each firm must carry a
sufficient safety stock for all ten items to decrease vulnerability to stock
outages. All of these firms must ship in less-than-carload quantities, which
results in excessively high distribution costs. Also, since they are competing
with each other, sales personnel costs, advertising costs, and additional
marketing costs must be borne at a high level by all. If by some means (e.g.,

ITEMS

FIRMS	1	2	3	4	5	6	7	8	9	10	SUPPLY
1	X	X	X	X	X	X	X	X	X	X	S_1
2	X	X	X	X	X	X	X	X	X	X	S_2
3	X	X	X	X	X	X	X	X	X	X	S_3
4	X	X	X	X	X	X	X	X	X	X	S_4
5	X	X	X	X	X	X	X	X	X	X	S_5
6	X	X	X	X	X	X	X	X	X	X	S_6
7	X	X	X	X	X	X	X	X	X	X	S_7
8	X	X	X	X	X	X	X	X	X	X	S_8
9	X	X	X	X	X	X	X	X	X	X	S_9
10	X	X	X	X	X	X	X	X	X	X	S_{10}
DEMAND	D_1	D_2	D_3	D_4	D_5	D_6	D_7	D_8	D_9	D_{10}	Total

FIGURE 7.1. The Nonoptimal Producers: Ten Items Made by Ten Firms

Japan's use of trading company guidance) all ten firms can be persuaded (and allowed) to specialize so that each firm has a different item (among the ten items), then special-purpose equipment can be justified and will lead to the most efficient continuous flow-shop work configuration with significantly lower per unit production costs. This is illustrated in Figure 7.2.

With flow-shop volume, the reject rate decreases, while quality consistency improves along with quality level. Both types of quality enhancement lead to lower market price elasticity, which is relevant to marketing productivity. Continuing with the list of advantages gained by specialization, each firm now garners quantity discounts on materials. Safety stock inventory levels can be decreased as a result of having more customers for fewer items. Carload quantity shipments are achieved at lower per unit distribution costs. Selling costs can be reduced because media can be purchased at discounts, promotion costs can be decreased, and the sales organization be-

ITEMS

FIRMS	1	2	3	4	5	6	7	8	9	10	SUPPLY
1	x										S_1
2		x									S_2
3			x								S_3
4				x							S_4
5					x						S_5
6						x					S_6
7							x				S_7
8								x			S_8
9									x		S_9
10										x	S_{10}
DEMAND	D_1	D_2	D_3	D_4	D_5	D_6	D_7	D_8	D_9	D_{10}	Total

FIGURE 7.2.   Ten Optimal Producers: Each Firm Specializing in One Item

comes specialized. Thus, a system of interacting, positively reinforcing effects operates to decrease costs so that lower prices can be charged for higher quality items. *There is net social gain.*

The optimal producer is not necessarily a monopolist. There can be more than one efficient flow shop if the technology and market demand permit. Nevertheless, the notion of the optimal producer may run afoul of antitrust laws that should be reevaluated in terms of post-1950 process capabilities. The old belief that returns to scale are insignificant in comparison with the evils of monopoly power should be reexamined. In a study entitled "Why Innovations Fail," Myers and Sweezy state, "The assumption that an innovation will violate antitrust regulations may prevent its development" (1978, p. 45). This effect should also be taken into account.

A variety of methods exists for increasing output volume without reference to existing demand levels. Some of these are illustrated in Figure 7.3. It should be noted, however, that the optimal producer's ability to lower costs while raising quality may very well increase demand, a situation generally to the good.

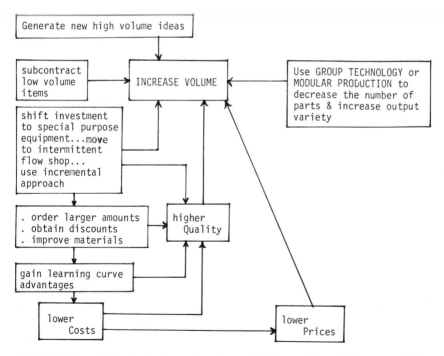

FIGURE 7.3. Methods for Increasing Output Volume without Reference to Existing Demand Levels

7.7. GREATER RELIANCE ON METHODOLOGICAL INNOVATION

Even before the Industrial Revolution, technological change always required some degree of methodological innovation. For example, the Jacquard loom (perfected by 1804) involved new ways to assign and to schedule work. However, until Frederick W. Taylor, little was heard about the importance of the methods for doing work. Taylor, Gantt, and many others developed appropriate methodology for improving project management and for scheduling work in the job shop, based upon well-designed jobs. Industrial engineering was responsible for a succession of methodological improvements over the first half of the twentieth century. The fields of operations research and management science joined ranks with industrial engineering after World War II to utilize existing technology in the most productive methodological fashion.

In spite of major contributions, methodological innovation has never received the same level of publicity as technological innovation. For example, we have all read a great deal about technological diffusion, but little has been written about methodological diffusion, the effect of which can be considerable (see Starr, 1971). The important point is that technological innovation is not the only kind of innovation that can improve productivity. Furthermore, whereas technological change requires increased capital investment, methodological improvement produces savings that are often there for the taking. For example, using linear programming, refineries over the world have substantially increased the productivity of their facilities.

In the 1980s, strong methodological capabilities exist for all types of work configurations. In fact, every day the potential for greater productivity increases with further developments in project management of the critical path, linear programming, applications that require integer solutions or stochastic conditions, queueing approaches to bottlenecked systems, and savings obtained from better management of inventories, improved line-balancing methods, distribution and facility-location decisions, and so forth.

Given that a job shop is the necessary work configuration, methods exist for solving in sequence the aggregate scheduling problem, followed by shop-loading decisions, and ultimately the detailed sequencing rules for doing the job. Savings of 10 to 30 percent can be realized by conscientiously employing appropriate methodology. Similarly, it is generally accepted that PERT-type project management can prevent cost overruns of 50 percent that were typical of the pre-PERT era, as explained by Kossiakoff (1960, p. 109). The employment of inventory methodology will generally produce savings that far outstrip the cost of the initial study and the costs of maintaining the system.

Since such effective methodology exists to improve productivity, why is it not fully utilized? Previously, we have described the resistance to change of a typical production department. This applies to new methodology, as well as to new technology. Furthermore, to be effective, methodological innovation requires continuous maintenance. The dynamics of the production, market, and distribution-system factors can quickly outdate the best of work. Consequently, a permanent support system is required for effective methodological innovation. Because of its narrow, cost-cutting orientation, the production department does not attempt to secure sufficient budget to achieve these objectives.

When the systemwide benefits of new methods are highlighted, it is frequently easier to get the needed support, as, for example, when the marketing department observes the benefits of improved inventory control obtained by using material requirements planning (MRP). This is also a management information system, and support may be forthcoming from that organizational area as well.

An aggressive company attempting to move toward a flow-shop configuration from a typical job-shop situation manages to achieve larger batches of work. This permits amortization of setup charges against a greater number of units. Previous work schedules must be changed. Old inventory analyses must be revamped. Eventually, large enough batches of work will have been aggregated so that an intermittent flow shop can be used. Equipment must be changed, and new scheduling algorithms applied. The intermittent flow shop yields reduced costs per unit of work but requires capital investments above the job-shop level, yet below the full-fledged flow shop.

It is in this range of more than a job shop and less than a flow shop that methodology is called upon to provide optimal procedures for work scheduling, inventory management, and quality control. Errors can be very costly because the production volumes are high. It should be noted that when new designs are run through a flow shop, as the automobile industry does on a yearly basis, an intermittent flow shop exists. In the start-up months, such a work configuration is particularly vulnerable to faulty design and assembly, which can result in costly repair callback charges to remedy dangerous defects. With careful testing based on exhaustive planning, the number of such errors can be substantially reduced. Error reduction is yet another way in which methodology can be used to improve productivity.

The increased reliance on methodology is accompanied by the availability of increasingly powerful and less costly computers. The price tag for bridging the gap between production methods currently practiced and those that promise increased productivity continues to drop every year. Thus, an ever larger number of organizations can afford high productivity.

7.8. THE ACHIEVEMENT OF RENEWABLE GROWTH

To achieve the suggested changes in work configurations will require many social and governmental innovations to absorb and to utilize existing technological and methodological capabilities. Operating against these renewable growth policies are the following:

The mental set of production managers who do not like to "rock the boat" and who pioneered in making job-shop systems effective during and after World War II; these production managers are cost conscious but not aware of demand/supply elasticity effects;

The mental set of marketing managers who assume that production managers will find the most effective way to produce;

All managers' reluctance to give up market share, even when it is barely profitable;

Union managers' fears of fewer jobs and the existing antitrust climate.

What might be done about these forces that dampen and quench renewable productivity growth? The use of *modular production* and *group technology* are at the head of the class because they permit gradual achievement of flow shops that have job-shop variety in their outputs. In addition, we must do the following:

Elevate the status of production managers;

Encourage systems thinking; first, disseminate the advantage of life-cycle planning for product-line evolution, and, second, infuse production decisions with marketing and distribution factors, and similarly build production considerations into marketing decisions; instead of solely emphasizing increased demand, the concept of changing the production configuration to improve productivity for existing demand must be instilled;

Make it hard for marginal production items to survive by taxing low profit items; the marketing situation of selling nonoptimal production quantities by dint of being somewhat profitable should be recognized as being socially wasteful;

Reward R&D for process innovation as much as for product innovation; rewrite patent laws so they promote improved productivity; find additional ways to help subsidize an increased willingness for risk taking; support life-cycle planning to prevent high productivity from stifling innovation;

Concentrate on aggregating volume; tax incentives could be used to motivate managers to achieve lower per unit costs; especially, promote research on how to elevate service productivity;

Pay workers for a reasonable part of the advantages gained from the flow shop, and educate everyone about the mutual benefits;

Study the trading company concept developed by the Japanese to increase output volumes, often labeled Japan, Inc.

There is no higher valued job in society than that of production manager. When that is recognized, there will no longer be a productivity problem. Instead, the United States can experience economic renaissance.

REFERENCES

Abernathy, William J., 1979, *The Productivity Dilemma,* Baltimore: Johns Hopkins University Press.

Booz, Allen and Hamilton, 1979, "Merging Industrial Operations and Corporate Strategy," *Outlook,* January.

Boston Consulting Group, 1979, "Winning the Game with a Hot Theory," *New York Times,* April 15, Section 3, pp. F1, F4.

Dogramaci, A., 1979, "Design of Common Components considering Implications of Inventory Costs and Forecasting," *AIIE Transactions,* vol. 11, no. 2, June, pp. 1–7.

Haynes, Frederick L., 1976, "Productivity: The Changing Challenge," *Industrial Engineering,* March, pp. 34–37.

Kendrick, John W., 1979, "Sources of Productivity Growth and of the Recent Slow-Down," in the study of the New York Stock Exchange *Reaching a Higher Standard of Living.* Address requests to: Dr. William C. Freund, Office of Economic Research, New York Stock Exchange, Inc., 11 Wall Street, New York, N.Y. 10005.

Knayer, Manfred, 1970, "Group Technology: A New Approach to Manufacturing," *Industrial Engineering,* September, pp. 23–27.

Kossiakoff, A., 1960, "The Systems Engineering Process," in *Operations Research and Systems Engineering,* edited by Charles D. Flagle et al., Baltimore: Johns Hopkins University Press.

McConnell, Campbell R., 1979, "Keeping Informed," *Harvard Business Review,* March–April, pp. 16–25.

Malkiel, Burton G., 1979*a*, "The Capital Formation Problem in the United States," *Journal of Finance,* vol. 34, no. 2, May, pp. 291–306.

_____, 1979*b*, "Productivity—the Problem behind the Headlines," *Harvard Business Review,* May–June, pp. 17–27.

Myers, Sumner, and Eldon E. Sweezy, 1978, "Why Innovations Fail," *Technology Review,* March/April, pp. 40–46.

Starr, Martin K., 1973, "Productivity Is the U.S.A.'s Problem,"*California Management Review,* vol. 16, no. 2, Winter, pp. 32–36.

_____, 1971, "The Transfer of Public Administration Methodology," *Interregional Seminar on the Use of Modern Management Techniques in the Public Administration of Developing Countries,* vol. 2, Technical Papers, New York: United Nations, pp. 86–99.

_____, 1965, "Modular Production—a New Concept," *Harvard Business Review,* vol. 43, no. 6, November–December, pp. 131–140.

8 PRODUCTIVITY AND ORGANIZATION MANAGEMENT

Leo B. Moore and Christine B. Moore

8.1. INTRODUCTION

Whenever an array of productivity figures, charts, or graphs is displayed to show performance, rest assured that in the final analysis, someone was responsible for those results. Moreover, it is also to be expected that someone interested in those results will judge and decide on the state of the depicted performance because that is the purpose of the review. Productivity is a measure of how well people are responding to the understood objectives and accepted goals of an enterprise.

In its basic definition of "the ratio of output to input," productivity simply asks the question, What did people produce for what they used? On a broader basis, productivity assesses the effectiveness of the allocation of both technical and human resources, as well as the efficiency of their utilization. Even more broadly, there are those who feel that productivity should include some measure of the health and well-being of people, in the sense of their leading productive working lives and careers, with personal objectives that relate to those of the enterprise (Sutermeister, 1976).

Contributions to productivity arise from the relative state of the technology employed and the basic values of the administrative practices pursued, together with the interaction of people as they live and work in the enterprise. Ultimately, productivity is a test of the competence, discipline, and dedication of management, made evident by the exercise of wise planning, effective coordination, authentic communication, and adequate control. The response to that test is found in the ability, initiative, and willingness of every member of the enterprise to contribute constructively to its performance through the elimination of nonproductive efforts. Although technical improvements will always be the source of significant productivity increases, these are always made possible by people, influencing both their inception and their application, as well as their ultimate effectiveness. The reaction that people exhibit toward technical innovation is influenced by the managerial philosophy inherent in the administration of the organization. The manager sets the tone to which people respond.

In this vein, management responsible for productivity decides what the objective will be, whether at the lowest level of generally acceptable performance or at some higher level. The degree of performance may reflect internal constraints, such as the nature of the enterprise, government regulations, customer requirements, union relations, or monetary controls, and external considerations, such as the culture of the environment, national employment policy, or changing demographics of the world. But primarily, the decision is made by members of management who take courses of action that relate to that decision. Generally, management will follow a process of building for expected performance and then changing the purpose of the enterprise toward new expectations in order to reach an ever higher level of productivity.

The decision that is reached applies to organizations of all kinds, although specific organizations will present particular problems—for example, measurement. The great increase in the number of people who process information rather than build product would be such a case. Concern for productivity should always be a pressing matter since resources required by every enterprise are scarce and costly and should be conserved and employed properly.

Finally, there are organizations, both public and private, that are distinguished by their recognized superior accomplishments. In the area of productivity, their example and experience are as important as the findings from appropriate research studies. Learning how to attain both expected and improved performance as a continuing, dynamic managerial effort is an unending, challenging task.

8.2. TECHNICAL PROGRESS

Under proper conditions, the human mind readily turns to technical solutions of pressing problems and continues to probe for improved solutions in the form of better materials, methods, or devices. As a consequence, quantum leaps in productivity as measured by worldly goods always have been made, and will continue to be made, through technical invention, development, and improvement. The recognition of opportunity, the freedom to experiment, and the right to fail are essential to success in these activities.

Throughout its history, the United States has had a tradition and has been a prime example of the creative urge for inventive problem solving. Starting, for example, with the work of Eli Whitney, the 1800s produced a tidal wave of creative engineering. Although Whitney is better known for his invention of the cotton gin and its contribution to the cotton industry, he pioneered the development of mass production techniques that spread throughout the industrial scene in the manufacture of such diverse items as clocks and tinware. The impact was felt in every corner of the country in an exciting search for new materials, tools, machines, and equipment, as well as new production and manufacturing techniques. These in some combination formed the basis for new enterprises of every description and changed the nature of existing ones. When Henry Ford used Whitney's techniques, he made the automobile available to everyone of modest means. When Charles F. Kettering developed the first practical self-starter, he put every woman behind the wheel of a car. And so development continues in computers, watches, and calculators, as well as in lasers and satellites, to maintain an established American tradition for material productivity as a national mark of distinction. As other countries are similarly urged, that reputation and that mark serve as a challenge in the satisfaction of the productivity needs of the world as a whole.

While the continuing value of the technical approach to productivity is fundamental in the production of material things, the concepts of engineering also established and continue to influence management practices. In the field of organization, Fredrick Taylor and his followers have made significant contributions down through the years. Unfortunately, his work became dubbed as "scientific management," and he became known as a "time-study man" and his followers as "efficiency engineers." In fact, Taylor was a competent researcher who brought discipline and creativity to the study of the management of work. Out of his studies, there developed the concepts and techniques of work planning and scheduling, methods and time study, employee training and development, coordination and control, and other matters considered fundamental management activities. Thus, the logic and creativity of engineering as a discipline will always be an important contributor to productivity and its management. Never is this so true as when a manager assumes a new responsibility.

8.3. THE RATIONAL/ADAPTABLE ORGANIZATION

Following engineering logic, every manager in the natural act of planning and organizing will inevitably build a basic organization or work bureaucracy. Not unlike a design engineer working on a new product, the manager, in his or her primary concern for results, will construct a mechanism that provides assurance of promised performance. This mechanism is the bureaucracy. It includes the accumulation of knowledge and skill, experience and wisdom, and practice and technique that management strives to assemble in order to minimize failure. As the first order of business, the course of this action is indeed sensible because it reduces the need to reinvent the wheel by employing with confidence what is already known. It is also realistic because it establishes early the organizational problems that need to be solved in order to meet the insistent demand for timely, acceptable performance.

One cannot challenge the essential logic of this approach to getting the job done nor the logical process it provides of organizing to do the work. As set forth by Brown (1974), it provides the theme for organizing as follows: listing the work elements that must be performed, combining them into suitable task units, and joining them together into jobs that can be described and specified. Thus, the jobs are organized and their interrelationships established in a hierarchy of fulfillment of performance, both at the employee and the managerial levels. With this resultant triangular arrangement on paper, the task is simply to find, select, and train people to fill those particular jobs, with the assurance that their individual performances will add up to total performance of the enterprise.

In organizing efforts, a manager is wisely guided by the traditional best practice that exists in similar organizations. Such organizations have learned how to be adaptable in a rational way to the demands they face. In manufacturing, shoe companies are product-oriented to respond to the changing market; refineries are process-oriented to accommodate the needs of the technology. Also, in other functional areas, good reasons usually exist for the way the work is organized. Managers may decide to perform the work differently (for example, selling cosmetics door-to-door), but when they do, they should look for guidance in their organizing activities to organizations that have that particular experience.

In the resultant work bureaucracy, not only is the hierarchy of jobs paramount; it also defines the hierarchy of the people who hold those jobs, establishes the authority and responsibility possessed by the job holder, states the nature and level of competence required, and in written documentation sets practices and procedures that relate one job to another. The effect is to establish a separation of technical competence and a technique of control of work activity that in combination will assure achievement of the goals of the enterprise. The practice holds whether it involves fighting fires, tending the sick, or delivering the mail. Whatever else may be said about the bureaucracy, it gets the work done.

This underlying concept that every enterprise in its line organization has a basic work bureaucracy designed to assure its primary performance is important for two reasons. First, there are thousands of essentially bureaucratic organizations with relatively productive records. These stand on their ability to perform and add to their knowledge, skill, and expertise by successfully solving operational problems when they arise. They maintain their productive presence in the world of work on these grounds alone. Second, from this group there will emerge those enterprises that, for purposeful reason, decide to raise their productivity sights above the level of primary performance. Here, the strength of both structure and practice provided by the basic organization to the enterprise is needed to endorse and support this decision.

8.4. CHANGING PURPOSE

The process of building the basic work organization is a satisfying managerial task because in and of itself it is a productive one. Something now exists to perform where previously there was none. This is the thrill that an entrepreneur experiences, as does everyone who works long and hard to bring an idea to fruition, to solve the problems of the day, to sense achievement and recognition in the challenge of the job, or to establish finally a viable entity. Thus, in the due course of time, some degree of stability is reached, and the bureaucracy is in place.

When management decides to raise the level of productivity, the decision should represent more than good intentions. It should be clearly seen as a change in the purpose of the organization—not a rejection of the work bureaucracy but an addition to it of a new dimension. Added to the rational and adaptable organization is the requirement of improved performance in some measurable terms. What these terms should be will depend on the nature of the enterprise.

While the decision to change the purpose of the organization is a clear exercise of managerial leadership, management must understand how the change involves others. Management may say that they sense expanded opportunity, broader services, or competitive strengths, but these conclusions must be supported in the marketplace. Satisfied customers have the greatest impact on purpose when they call for increased service, greater variety, or newer efforts. The combination of responsive management with an appreciative market is essential to changing purpose, but this is only part, albeit the exciting part, of the total change.

Previously, the work organization dealt mainly with needs, the needs of individuals, customers, employees, investors, and suppliers, in personal terms. The changed purpose sensed by management that wants a better enterprise and by customers who want better service means that the enterprise will now be dealing with wants, the wants of groups that see in improved productivity the satisfaction both of their needs and their wants. Or at least, that is their expectation. Having demonstrated its ability to perform, the enterprise might then be expected to perform better. This is called progress.

Therefore, the decision to improve productivity must eventually be in terms of the wants of the various groups that place trust and confidence in the enterprise and its management, as well as their hopes for its improved performance. To satisfy these demands—of investors for return, employees for working conditions, customers for service, community for citizenship—management must add to the basic organization to accomplish its added purpose and add to its own competence to improve its productivity.

8.5. THE COMPETITIVE/PROGRESSIVE ORGANIZATION

To the line organization, the call for improved productivity simply means that help will be required in solving problems, particularly technical problems. Using the bureaucratic approach, this help will be provided by establishing staff groups in functional areas, such as research and development in engineering, industrial engineering in manufacturing, product development in marketing, and systems engineering in administration. The concept of staff, borrowed from the military, places upon the staff the responsibility of providing specialized knowledge and skill, undertaking appropriate studies, and furnishing recommendations to the line as to possible courses of action.

In addition, the line will want to provide professional help for organization-wide activities, such as purchasing and personnel. Thus, personnel will strive to hire better people and to train and develop them for improved performance. Also, specialized techniques might well be organized, such as value engineering in purchasing, quality assurance in manufacturing, and computer programming and modeling for financial and operational control, as improved aids to technical problem solving. Taken together, these are all designed to provide organized effectiveness to the work bureaucracy.

However, in spite of the excellence of technical aids and of professional problem solving, improved productivity proves to be a continuing struggle. For further help, management will from time to time mount organization-wide programs aimed at specific performance goals, such as cost reduction, waste elimination, and safety improvement. The purpose of these special efforts is to highlight the need for concerted action of all members of the enterprise toward the desired goal. To show their interest, management will often provide strong support through publicity efforts, as well as a specific target, such as zero defects as a quality objective. Inevitably, in the process of introducing new methods, practices, or procedures, managers discover that subordinates present ideas of their own about how the work might be done; as a result, the organization will establish a suggestion system that permits people to put their ideas into writing and submit them to management for approval.

For thousands of enterprises organized for competitive and progressive performance, effectiveness at a relatively high but varying level is the general experience. For management, improved productivity proves to be a constant challenge that demands continuing attention. Organized effectiveness, for example, presents to management basic issues in at least three areas. First, the nature of the relationship of the staff to the line requires clear definition. In the line bureaucracy, the staff is viewed as subordinate and helping. As a result, the staff too often becomes immersed in current line problems to the neglect of their own responsibilities toward the future; industrial engineering is working on quality problems caused by material variations, or research and development is redesigning existing products to meet changes in customer specifications. As temporary measures, such practices are easily justified, but they can become relatively permanent. Second, productivity programs tend to become fads that fade unless given determined and continued line support, even though the goals of these programs, such as safety improvement, are clearly valuable and worthwhile. Third, new management practices, introduced to improve productivity, need to be tailored to each specific organization and require more care in their introduction and implementation. The widespread willingness to buy or to borrow a new practice because it promises improved productivity is not usually effective.

But the real problem that emerges in the competitive and progressive enterprise is the apparent willingness of management, strongly oriented to the logic and discipline of engineering, to leave largely untapped the potential of its people for contributions to productivity.

8.6. CHANGING VALUES

In his role of supervisor, every manager must face the question of dependability of performance of both individuals and groups. Even though he has employed all the logic, discipline, and experience that he could muster and sought the advice of staff professionals, he realizes that his decisions finally rest on the performance of others. That performance often seems inconsistent and unpredictable. Some individuals with splendid credentials fail miserably; others with less promising backgrounds succeed beyond belief. In the same way, group performance varies throughout the organization. As a result, every manager devotes considerable time and energy to this perplexing dilemma and concludes that while there may be some basic useful knowledge, he must understand his particular situation and its own contingent dimensions when dealing with performance problems.

In his search for understanding, the thoughtful manager will review and study the many decisions that have an impact on the human side of enterprise. Out of these efforts, there will arise two concerns—one for the environment of the organization and the other for the feelings of its members. The performance of any organization can be better understood when seen as the interaction of these two dimensions. While not abandoning their basic principles, managers have in the course of history been willing to experiment with aspects of environment, such as structure, style, communication, and job design. More difficult to cope with are such expressed feelings as the work ethic is dead, people want to do their thing, and people are entitled to have more meaningful work and to live fuller lives. Most likely these ideas have always been true, but management has shown an increased willingness to listen to opinions and feelings, both subordinated by the logical and factual approach to decisions. This willingness has been encouraged by management support of researchers and consultants, both internal and external, whose work, particularly after World War II, has reached such proportions and range of content as to confirm for the manager that the problem is indeed serious and complex, and demanding. For example, Stogdill (1974), in his recent survey of leadership theory and research, analyzed over 3000 books and articles, a bibliography that required 150 pages. The question for the manager is whether the volume and diversity of the literature contains principles, techniques, and practices that might aid performance and productivity.

While that literature is widely ranging, often confusing, and sometimes conflicting, most managers believe that it is important to understand its content and implications. For example, in the area of organizational structure, the usual result of a manager's organizing efforts is a tall, triangular pyramid. Raising the question of decentralizing in order to improve communication and control as aides to productivity might suggest creating a flat structure by removing layers of organization between the executive and unit managers, as in a chain of hotels, restaurants, or stores. In the opposite direction, a functional organization overwhelmed with priority problems might consider the use of the matrix, which is an overlay of specific assignments—for example, product managers in marketing or project managers in engineering. These managers draw personnel from functional areas according to need and are thus able to control progress and performance through effectiveness of allocation of resources and their supervision.

The concept that organization is only a tool in the hands of the manager shows its relationship to the manager's style. Drawing from a continuum, such as MacGregor's (1960) Theory X and Y, the manager strives to establish a mode of operation described in some fashion, such as the Managerial Grid (Blake and Mouton, 1968) or Likert's (1967) System 1 through 4, to promote productive performance through motivation, such as is best described by Maslow's (1968) needs hierarchy. This approach seems supported by Herzberg's (1966) inquiry into job satisfaction and by Myers's (1970) work in Texas Instruments, which concluded that achievement, responsibility, recognition, and the job itself lead to productivity.

In the matter of job design, the recognition of the potential of educated, trained personnel to handle more demanding tasks and to improve productivity received media attention at Volvo, AT&T, and General Foods under the encouraging title of job enrichment. Thirty years earlier, similar efforts at IBM's typewriter plant in Poughkeepsie, New York, and Maytag's washing machine plant in Newton, Iowa, were labeled job enlargement. These earlier endeavors were experimental approaches that showed the need to include the related costs of recruitment, training, absenteeism, turnover, promotion, and rate of product change in job design decisions. The failure to employ the full potential of an employee might involve more than establishing work opportunities for educated and trained personnel.

Nevertheless, the general concern for productivity in an era of rising inflation prompted a review of the quality of working life by a congressional committee, whose chief recommendation was for improved communication of employees and management through joint meetings about mutual problems (*Work in America,* 1973). This idea has been the basis of union-management cooperation for some time. As the representative of employees, the union movement has from its inception been concerned about the level of satisfaction that its members receive in the work place. Taylor, in his preoccupation with engineering logic, could not comprehend the concerns of the machinists union and its continual attempt to communicate how its members felt about their work. There were those followers of Taylor who realized the importance of the human element, but the great success of Taylor's basic work overshadowed this concern, and the overshadowing was confirmed by the culture of the day. After World War I, Williams (1967), working among laborers in steel mills and mines, clearly saw not only the great security of just having a job, but also the significant need for a sense of pride in the work itself and for recognition from the supervisor and from fellow employees of competent performance. Mayo (Gellerman, 1963), analyzing an engineering experiment that investigated the level of light supplied to employees for work, realized in that Hawthorne experience that people wanted to make their work meaningful by producing to the perceived expectations of others. Mogensen (1932) had demonstrated extensively the value of working with people to improve the productivity of their work and at the same time to help them feel the importance of their contribution. Indications are, as they always have been, that people feel about what they do, especially their job, as a way to feel better about themselves. But they want their own opinion confirmed by someone who counts, especially their supervisor.

The importance of communication—fuller, broader, wider—in the life and productivity of every organization cannot be denied. It is a predictable outcome of all opinion surveys and is confirmed completely through survey feedback. Failure of communication is a major cause for the formation of informal groups that, like their formal counterparts, possess in their cohesiveness the power to influence productivity positively or negatively. For these reasons, the understanding of group dynamics is important in the role of manager.

Normally, groups are seen as a resistive force in the management of productivity. In the extreme, the power of the union to shut down productivity completely with a strike is well known, but less understood is the practice of restricting output, the inordinate delay of action, and the general disenchantment with work. All these conditions may be found among managers and employees alike. But they most generally exist in a period of change and are broadly labeled "resistance."

Even if the change may be factually proven to be beneficial, people will resist it when they view it with resentment, fear, or insecurity. Their resistance will be markedly higher when they feel that the change has been imposed upon them by the arbitrary actions of others. Two ways exist for reducing such resistance, both related. One is extensive communication with concerned individuals and their groups about the proposed change and its consequences. The other is the involvement of concerned people in the formulation or application of the change. These two actions are the foundation of what has come to be known as participative management. While resistance is an important aspect of managing productivity, it should be more properly viewed as a problem of communication and motivation.

In an effort to improve productivity, many organizations have embraced a combination of ideas known generally as management by objectives. Every enterprise has some sense of objective for the long term and some clearer concept of goals for the short run, but often these are not sharply defined and therefore not openly communicated. By deciding upon objectives and related goals that are clear, challenging, attainable, measurable, and realistic, the productivity of an organization will benefit from a better understanding of its purpose through open communication and the resultant motivation to meet these aims. This will especially be true if the objectives and goals are the result of participative processes throughout the organization. However, many enterprises have experienced difficulties following this practice. Generally, these cases reveal the need to develop competence in planning, to review their management information system, and to establish an environment of authentic communication and skill in conflict situations.

For those who investigate problems of this type with a concern for the psychology and sociology of work, their studies and findings, as well as their recommendations and interventions, have come under the umbrella term of *organization development* (OD). OD embraces a host of individuals who have developed approaches and techniques that have the avowed purpose of changing the human conditions in organizations, developing ability to cope with increasing change, and improving productivity (Bennis, 1969). There is no question that the extensive OD endeavors have been in their own way beneficial in seeking new managerial knowledge and particularly in probing the human side of enterprise. If hopes are realized, these efforts will contribute to more effective management of human resources as true assets. For example, in the personnel function, specific concern must be shown for the effectiveness of established techniques of performance appraisal, training and education for personal development, and career planning and progress. Studies of particular OD efforts do reveal positive results, at least on some short-term basis in accordance with the Hawthorne effect. General reports indicate enthusiasm for the aims of these endeavors, but there have been some notable failures (Mirvis, 1977).

As an educational intervention aimed at developing attitudes appropriate to manager development, OD seems broadly accepted. With regard to contribution to performance, those cases of failure suggest concern on the part of managers for an apparent attack upon the basic structure, practices, and procedures of the work bureaucracy, particularly by the external consultant. Clearly, the important contributions of OD efforts generally rest on the better understanding of human relationships in an organizational setting. The most important part of that understanding is the willingness and ability to deal with feelings. Facts have long been the mainstay of managing; feelings have always been just as important. Managers must learn how to manage with feelings, as well as with facts, in mind. Certainly, this is an explicit necessity for managers who wish to build an enterprise devoted to ever increasing productivity.

8.7. THE INNOVATING/IMPROVING ORGANIZATION

At this level of productivity, the management of the enterprise, having an organization that provides consistent performance that is competitive and progressive, decides to be among the leaders in its field, if not The Leader. From the experience of such leaders, the managers see the need to build an environment of continual improvement, as distinguished from the environment of competitive performance that currently exists. It is recognized that this effort will be broadly based, meaning that all aspects of the enterprise will respond to the requirements of increasing productivity and will be subject to scrutiny. The theme of this dynamic dimension in the organization will be *progress on purpose* (Graham and Parvis, 1979).

Such a decision should not be taken lightly. Many organizations have attempted to reach this level, making forays into its domain. Even though they attain markedly good results, many have failed to establish the effort as a permanent, ongoing style of operation because of lack of persistence. There must be available some appropriate amounts of resources in people, time, and money to be treated as an investment. Continuing efforts must be supported by an alert management group, disciplined and determined to make that investment. For the managers, there will be the need to study and to learn how to cope with the unique challenge of creativity, innovation, and change as special managerial tasks in their particular enterprises by drawing upon well-established research findings and converting this knowledge to their own unique situations.

8.8. CREATIVE ENVIRONMENT

The definition of creativity is simply the process of generating ideas, completely free of judgment, evaluation, or criticism. Ideation is an emotional process; the product, the idea, is intellectual. Both the process and product are extremely sensitive to assessment, except by the individual engaged in the process. The creative environment is built on open communication about ideas, about having ideas, and about how the ideas arose.

The manager must recognize that everyone has ideas, particularly about his or her own job and its dimensions. An important part of the manager's job is to encourage people's potential for creativity. People want to talk about their ideas and will, if given an opportunity. They want their ideas given consideration and, where possible, used in a constructive fashion. The task for the manager is to develop the discipline to listen with these concepts in mind.

In the creative environment, the supervisor seeks ideas by asking individuals or small groups for their thoughts and feelings. This is in sharp contrast to the environment of performance in which communication generally involves problems and difficulties that are judged to be interferences. These on-the-spot decisions, often termed *crisis management,* deal with barriers to be surmounted immediately. More often than not, any idea that is ventured as a possibility that does not represent past experience or immediate solution is slapped down as impractical. From these rejections, people learn to suppress their ideas. So, in building a creative environment, a manager in his supervisory role must take the time to build trust and confidence by providing support to the creative process. The best support of all would be the approval to use the idea as proposed. At the least, the manager must indicate an interest in additional thoughts and a willingness to consider the proposal and to talk about it further.

An important ingredient in a creative environment is a creative manager, which means a manager who is willing to think about his own job and talk about his ideas with his own supervisor or with the person he is grooming as his successor. The experience of the emotional dimension of ideation firsthand is important to the manager's understanding the need to protect the feelings of others through fostering a creative environment.

While studies of traits and characteristics of managers have never been more than suggestive, for the innovative organization they have clear significance (Steiner, 1965). Comparing the lists of traits of effective performers with those of creative individuals reveals common attributes, such as highly dedicated, hardworking, and persevering to the point of working long hours. Both effective performers and creative individuals are adaptable in their flexibility of action toward a strong sense of goal orientation. The remaining characteristics of a strong performer are those that an organization traditionally says it needs, such as having a solid educational base, being a logical decisionmaker and effective communicator, and having an image that fits a disciplined individual. However, the remaining items on the list for creative persons, such as strong intellectual curiosity, high problem sensitivity with the emphasis on problem definition, anti-authoritarianism, compulsion for praise, and a long history of being idea-oriented, are descriptive of potential areas of conflict for the manager who is oriented toward performance alone. Furthermore, the creative person's indifference to rules, incomplete communication, personal working hours, and similar extensions of these characteristics are matters that managers dedicated to performance generally will not tolerate. Yet a manager seeking to develop a creative environment and recognizing them as traits must not just tolerate these dimensions; he must also encourage and support them during periods of creativity. Such a manager will differentiate clearly between his supervisory role in search of performance and in search of improved performance as two separate and distinguishable tasks. While at first this concept may seem difficult, it is perfectly in agreement with the two separable functions performed by the two hemispheres of the human brain. This difference must be specifically recognized in the act of innovation.

8.9. INNOVATIVE PROCESS

The process of innovation is the adjustment of an idea to the reality of value (Levitt, 1963). Many ideas as first conceived represent an identification of a need. Thomas Edison's feeling of the need of an electric light reflected his concern for existing lighting. When he developed the first effective lamp, the question arose as to how it might be used effectively. This is the thrust of innovation.

Except for the case in which an individual has the freedom to innovate on his own, and these are rare cases, most initial ideas require discussion, consideration, and elaboration before their potential usefulness is developed. Depending on the scope of the idea and its application, this process calls for group action, ranging in size and type of membership according to the need of the situation. Examples of such groups are an application group of employees who will use the idea, a peer group to gain agreement and consensus, a resource group to provide professional knowledge and expertise, and an interest group to broaden communication and lessen resistance to the new.

These project groups or teams require of the manager the ability to understand and to provide for their creative needs on the assumption that in their operation they will exhibit the creative characteristics already described, such as arise from the need for freedom. However, through training, the teams should be provided with group techniques and guidelines to facilitate cooperative exchange, conflict resolution, problem solving, and creative techniques, such as brainstorming. While the size and composition of these teams is a matter of judgment, they should be regarded as small and temporary. The membership is selected from the functions and levels of the organization deemed important to the development of the idea and its use.

The output from these teams is always a recommendation to the manager for a plan of action. The group decides on the scope of the idea, its area of application, the resources required, the values expected in its use, the essential difficulties to be faced, the timing of the facets of the action plan, and any other concerns that they foresee. From their deliberations, the group presents to the manager a recommended course of action. His task is to review, to assess, and to decide; his deliberations involve political, budgetary, and strategic considerations.

8.10. PLANNED CHANGE

There will be very few instances in which the manager will be quickly able to reach his decision to act. Even some supposedly small internal matter handled creatively by a group of his supervisors might turn out to be an embarrassing decision for the manager because of ramifications elsewhere. The purpose of planning the proposed change is to try to anticipate objections, concerns, and resistances and to develop means for dealing with them. This process is always a test of the manager and a contribution to his personal development (Beckhard, 1969).

In reaching his decision, yes or no, a good starting place is a review of the areas affected by the recommendation, which will vary depending on its nature and scope. But even the smallest must be traced to its fullest extent. A change in a material specification or the design of a part may raise havoc in the service department. Certain obvious factors, such as budget, manpower, special services, and particularly their availability, must be considered. Drafting, design, or maintenance may already be running overtime. The timing of this proposal must be reviewed with respect to other activities, as well as the risks involved as seen by supervisors, peers, and subordinates. A conservative view of the estimated returns, benefits, or advantages is important as a manager considers the possibilities of failure and how it may be avoided (Likert and Likert, 1976).

Out of these deliberations, a more disciplined look at the recommended plan of action may be taken. Most important will be its communication content with special emphasis on the degree of involvement of others. The sequence of the action details will require review to assess their interaction, along with how progress will be measured and how the necessary follow-up will be performed. The nature of the support that will be needed should influence the type of controls that will be exercised. In addition, the form of final reporting should be determined, as well as the giving of recognition to all persons who were a part of the effort.

In this planning of change, the manager is really struggling with the issue of gaining what was promised and maintaining those gains once they are accomplished. He is trying to discover ways to build the new into the existing work organization—in other words, to make the gains operational.

8.11. REVIEW

Although the focus of most discussions of productivity is on the average worker's comparative output, in reality the responsibility for the level of productivity in any enterprise rests squarely on the shoulders of its management. While members of management may have sound reasons for their decision on the level of productivity to be attained, it is that decision and the means taken to implement it that have significant influence on the human side of enterprise. The decision establishes the culture and climate of the environment in which people live and work.

Organizational development might be the term that describes the process that management employs in building an organization for the successive levels of acceptable, progressive, and innovative performance. This building process requires of every manager increasing levels of competence, greater attention to the task of managing, and growing sensitivity to people as the true source and essence of productivity. Management can and does develop increasing skill in the employment of material, technical, and financial resources that are generally available to all, but the real challenge lies in unleashing the potential for performance that rests in people.

For every enterprise, its people are its unique resource. To tap this unique potential is the highest accomplishment of every manager. To listen to people, to hear their ideas, and to know their feelings are to understand their need for challenging achievement, common purpose, and recognized excellence. But it is the manager who either provides or denies the opportunity for fulfillment. People look to the manager who has the skill, the art, and willingness to encourage them to contribute in their own unique way. Every enterprise needs more people concerned about productivity, and an understanding, feeling manager will stimulate that concern toward positive action.

REFERENCES

Beckhard, Richard, 1969, *Organization Development: Strategies and Models,* Reading, Mass.: Addison-Wesley.

Bennis, Warren G., 1969, *Organizational Development,* Reading, Mass.: Addison-Wesley.

Blake, Robert, and Jane Mouton, 1968, *Corporate Excellence through Grid Organizational Development,* Houston: Gulf Publishing.

Brown, Alvin, 1974, *Organization of Industry,* Englewood Cliffs, N.J.: Prentice-Hall.

Gellerman, Saul W., 1963, *Motivation and Productivity,* New York: American Management Associations.

Graham, Ben S., and Parvin S. Titus, eds., 1979, *Total Participation for Productivity,* New York: American Management Associations.

Herzberg, Frederick, 1966, *Work and the Nature of Man,* Cleveland: World Publishing.

Levitt, Theodore, 1963, "Creativity Is Not Enough," *Harvard Business Review,* May–June, pp. 72–83.

Likert, Rensis, 1967, *The Human Organization,* New York: McGraw-Hill.

Likert, R., and J. G. Likert, 1976, *New Ways of Managing Conflict,* New York: McGraw-Hill.

MacGregor, Douglas, 1960, *The Human Side of Enterprise,* New York: McGraw-Hill.

Maslow, Abraham H., 1968, *Toward a Psychology of Being,* New York: Van Nostrand.

Mirvis, Philip H., and David N. Berg, 1977, *Failures in Organization Development and Change,* New York: Wiley-Interscience.

Morgensen, Allan H., 1932, *Common Sense Applied to Motion and Time Study,* New York: McGraw-Hill.

Myers, M. Scott, 1970, *Every Employee a Manager,* New York: McGraw-Hill.

Steiner, Gary A., ed., 1965, *Creative Organization,* Chicago: University of Chicago Press.

Stogdill, Ralph M., 1974, *Handbook of Leadership: A Survey of Theory and Research,* New York: Free Press.

Sutermeister, Robert A., 1976, *People and Productivity,* New York: McGraw-Hill.

Williams, Whiting, 1967, *America's Mainspring and the Great Society,* New York: Frederick Fell.

Work in America, 1973, Report of a Special Task Force to the Secretary of Health, Education and Welfare, Cambridge, Mass.: MIT Press.

NAME INDEX

169

SUBJECT INDEX